POTTER V. SHRACKLE
AND
THE SHRACKLE CONSTRUCTION COMPANY

Sixth Edition

POTTER V. SHRACKLE
AND
THE SHRACKLE CONSTRUCTION COMPANY

Sixth Edition

Kenneth S. Broun

Henry Brandis Professor of Law Emeritus
University of North Carolina School of Law

Frank D. Rothschild

Attorney at Law
Kilauea, Hawaii

Revision by Kenneth S. Broun and Frank D. Rothschild based upon the
original file created by Kenneth S. Broun as revised by James H. Seckinger

NATIONAL INSTITUTE FOR TRIAL ADVOCACY

Address inquiries to:

Reprint Permission
National Institute for Trial Advocacy
1685 38th Street, Suite 200

Boulder, CO 80301-2735
Phone: (800) 225-6482
Fax: (720) 890-7069
E-mail: permissions@nita.org

ISBN 978-1-60156-205-0

FBA 1205

14 13 12 11   10 9 8 7 6 5 4 3 2 1

Printed in the United States of America

CONTENTS

Acknowledgments

The authors would like to thank the following for their assistance in the creation of the photographs and video clips that come with this file: Craig Gilbert, general contractor (Charles Shrackle); Bobby Dudley, former contractor and now Kona lawyer (Jeffrey Potter); Bob Bissenette, commercial painter (James Marshall); Courtney Haas, realtor and yoga instructor (Cheryl Tobias); and especially Anne Slifkin, attorney and mediator, whose portrayal of Kathy Potter in the original version of this file (c. 1976) became part of NITA lore.

We are also deeply indebted to Juan Gonzalez III, Principal, and Jaime Jue, Senior Associate, in the Forensic department of KPMG LLP for their outstanding work in upgrading and enriching the experts portion of this file, including the reports and tables of Dr. Glenn and Dr. Buchanan, the Dyer memorandum, and other related materials.

INTRODUCTION

This is a wrongful death action brought in Nita State Court by Jeffrey T. Potter, as administrator of the estate of his deceased wife, Katherine, and in his own behalf, against Charles T. Shrackle and the Shrackle Construction Company. Potter claims that Shrackle negligently drove the company's pickup, striking Katherine Potter as she was crossing the street, causing her death. Potter claims that Shrackle was acting in the course of the Shrackle Construction Company's business at the time of the accident.

Shrackle admits striking Mrs. Potter, but claims that she was crossing in the middle of the street, rather than in the pedestrian crosswalk, and that she did not look before entering the street in the path of Mr. Shrackle's truck. Defendants deny that Shrackle was negligent and allege contributory negligence on the part of the deceased, Mrs. Potter.

The applicable law is contained in the proposed jury instructions set forth at the end of the file.

SPECIAL INSTRUCTIONS FOR USE AS A FULL TRIAL

ISSUES FOR TRIAL

This case file may be used for a full trial on the issue of liability only or on the issues of both liability and damages. If used solely for the issue of liability, the proposed jury instructions should be modified accordingly by the deletion of instructions 16 and 17.

WITNESSES

For the plaintiff:

Officer Michael Young

Marilyn Kelly

James Marshall

Jeffrey Potter

Daniel Sloan

Robert Glenn

For the defendant:

Charles Shrackle

Alice Mallory

Victoria Williams

Juanita Williams

Benjamin Grimson

Elizabeth Buchanan

A party need not call all of the persons listed as its witnesses. Any or all of the witnesses may be called by any party, subject to the limitations below. However, if a witness is to be called by a party other than the one for whom he or she is listed, the party for whom the witness is listed will select and prepare the witness.

Limitation on Witnesses:

Each party is limited to four witnesses.

For the plaintiff:

Daniel Sloan's testimony is stipulated. If the trial is on both liability and damages, Dr. Robert Glenn is available to testify and the testimony of James Marshall will be stipulated. If tried on the issue of liability alone, James Marshall is available to testify.

For the defendant:

The testimony of Benjamin Grimson is stipulated, as well as the information about his subsequent imprisonment. If the trial is on both liability and damages, Elizabeth Buchanan is available to testify, and the testimony of Juanita Williams will be stipulated.

REQUIRED STIPULATIONS

Where testimony is stipulated pursuant to the above instructions, the statement or deposition of the witness is admissible and may be impeached by other information in the file.

Defendant submitted a Request for Admissions with regard to the accuracy and authenticity of Exhibits 29, 30, 31, and 32. Plaintiff filed admissions to all four exhibits.

The formula for calculating how many feet per second a vehicle travels is to multiply the miles per hour by 1.47.

SUGGESTED TIME LIMITS FOR FULL TRIAL

Voir dire	10 minutes per side (5 minutes per attorney when teamed up)
Opening statement	15 minutes per side
Witness examination	100 minutes per side
Closing argument	20 minutes per side

IN THE CIRCUIT COURT OF
DARROW COUNTY, NITA
CIVIL DIVISION

Jeffrey T. Potter, the)
Administrator of the Estate)
of Katherine Potter, and)
Jeffrey T. Potter, individually,)
)   Complaint
        Plaintiffs,)
)
v.)
)
Charles T. Shrackle and)
The Shrackle Construction Company,)
)
        Defendants.)

Plaintiff, Jeffrey T. Potter, individually and as administrator of the Estate of Katherine Potter, complains against Defendants, Charles T. Shrackle and Shrackle Construction Company, as follows:

FIRST CLAIM FOR RELIEF

1. Plaintiff was, and still is, a resident of Darrow County, Nita.

2. Defendant Charles T. Shrackle was, and still is, a resident of Darrow County, Nita, and the Defendant Shrackle Construction Company was, and still is, doing business in Darrow County, Nita.

3. Katherine Potter died on December 4, 2010.

4. Plaintiff and Katherine Potter were married at the time of her death and had been married for twelve years.

5. Plaintiff has been duly appointed the Administrator of Katherine Potter's estate.

6. On November 30, 2010, at about 3:30 p.m., Katherine Potter was walking in an easterly direction across Mattis Avenue at the intersection of Mattis and Kirby Avenues in Nita City, Nita.

7. At this time and place Defendant Charles T. Shrackle was driving a 2001 Toyota pickup truck which struck Katherine Potter, causing her serious injuries and death as a result of such injuries on December 4, 2010.

8.   The truck driven by Defendant Charles T. Shrackle was owned by the Defendant Shrackle Construction Company, and at the time Katherine Potter was struck by the truck, Charles T. Shrackle was performing duties for and acting on behalf of the Shrackle Construction Company.

9.   Defendant Charles T. Shrackle was driving the Toyota pickup truck in a careless, negligent, and reckless manner, and in violation of his duties under Nita Revised Statutes 89-12(4)(2010) to exercise due care to avoid striking the pedestrian Katherine Potter who was then lawfully walking across the street.

10. Defendant Charles T. Shrackle carelessly, negligently, and in violation of Nita Revised Statutes 89-12(4)(2010) failed to keep a proper lookout, to heed the fact that Katherine Potter was crossing the street in the immediate path of his truck, or to take any action to avoid striking Katherine Potter.

11. Defendant Charles T. Shrackle carelessly, negligently, and in violation of Nita Revised Statutes 89-12(4)(2010) failed to give proper warning of the sudden and unexpected approach of his truck either by sounding the horn or giving any other signal or warning.

12. Defendant Charles T. Shrackle's negligence caused Katherine Potter to suffer severe physical and mental pain and suffering from the date such injuries were incur red on November 30, 2010, until her death on December 4, 2010.

13. Defendant Charles T. Shrackle's negligence caused Katherine Potter to incur reasonable expenses for medical, hospital, and surgical care, and the loss of wages from the time of the collision until her death, in the sum of $107,800.

14. Defendant Charles T. Shrackle's negligence caused Jeffrey T. Potter, as personal representative of the Estate of Katherine Potter, to incurreasonable funeral and burial expenses, in the sum of $16,500.

SECOND CLAIM FOR RELIEF

15. Plaintiff realleges paragraphs 1 through 11.

16. Defendant Charles T. Shrackle's negligence caused Jeffrey T. Potter, as the surviving spouse of Katherine Potter, to suffer damages for the loss of:

     (a)   The reasonable expected net income of Katherine Potter;

     (b)   Services, protection, care, and assistance of Katherine Potter, whether voluntary or obligatory, to Jeffrey T. Potter;

(c)   Society, companionship, comfort, guidance, kindly offices, and advice of Katherine Potter to Jeffrey T. Potter.

WHEREFORE, Plaintiff demands judgment against Defendants, jointly and severally, in an amount in excess of $50,000, together with interest thereon and his costs herein, and for such other relief as the Court deems just and proper.

JURY DEMAND

Plaintiff demands a trial by jury in this action.

MADDEN &JAMES

by

William James

Attorneys for Plaintiff
Suite 720, Nita Bank Building
Nita City, Nita 99994
(555) 555-0003

DATED: April 7, 2011

IN THE CIRCUIT COURT OF
DARROW COUNTY, NITA
CIVIL DIVISION

Jeffrey T. Potter, the Administrator of the Estate of Katherine Potter, and Jeffrey T. Potter, individually, Plaintiffs, v. Charles T. Shrackle and The Shrackle Construction Company, Defendants.	))))))))))))))	Answer

Defendants for their Answer to Plaintiff's Complaint:

1. Admit the allegations contained in paragraphs 1–5, 7–8.

2. Admit that on November 30, 2010, at or about 3:30 p.m., Katherine Potter was crossing Mattis Avenue somewhere near the intersection of Kirby and Mattis Avenues. Defendants deny all other allegations in paragraph 6

3. Deny the allegations contained in paragraphs 9–14, 16.

FIRST AFFIRMATIVE DEFENSE

4. Any injuries sustained or suffered by Katherine Potter at the time and place mentioned in the Complaint were caused, in whole or in part, or were contributed to, by the negligence of Katherine Potter and not by any negligence of Charles T. Shrackle.

SECOND AFFIRMATIVE DEFENSE

5. Katherine Potter violated Nita Revised Statutes 89-12(4)(2010) by failing to cross the street in the marked pedestrian crosswalk, to keep a proper lookout for vehicles using the roadway and to yield the right of way to any such vehicles.

WHEREFORE, Defendants demand that judgment be entered in favor of the Defendants with the costs and disbursements of this action.

PIERCE, JOHNSON & CLARK

by

James Barber
_____

Attorneys for Defendants
Nita National Bank Plaza
Nita City, Nita 99994
(555) 555-6207

DATED: May 6, 2011

SUMMARY OF DEPOSITION OF MARILYN J. KELLY

1   My name is Marilyn J. Kelly. I live at 1910 Elder Lane, Nita City 99992.
2

3   On November 30, 2010, I was driving my car on Mattis Avenue, traveling in a north-
4   easterly direction. I was in the lane of traffic closest to the east side of the street. At
5   approximately 3:20 p.m. I was stopped for a red light at the intersection of Mattis and
6   Kirby Avenues. I was first in line and was stopped just south of the crosswalk.
7

8   Just as I stopped, a small boy ran across the street from the west to east and barely
9   avoided being struck by a car making a left turn from Kirby onto Mattis heading south.
10 When he reached the sidewalk, I heard the crossing guard who was standing on the
11 southeast corner of the intersection speak to the boy and say something to the effect
12 of, "You have got to watch for cars."
13

14 Just then I saw a woman with dark hair dressed in a dark jacket with some color on it
15 and a dark skirt on the west side of Mattis Avenue. She was just stepping off the curb
16 and starting to cross the street when I saw her. At that time the woman was walking at a
17 normal gait and was not running. She was definitely in the crosswalk, and I saw her take
18 two or three steps.
19

20 I then glanced back up at the light, and at that time I heard a thud. I looked up and saw
21 the woman flying through the air and then land with arms outstretched on the front of
22 the truck. She then went backward as if doing a backward somersault and fell under the
23 truck. She didn't complete a somersault, but just flew back and landed with her head
24 smashing on the pavement. At that time I thought to myself, "My God, stop, don't run
25 over her again." The truck driver appeared to be looking around immediately after the
26 impact as though looking to see what he had hit.
27

28 The truck stopped at a point approximately forty feet south of the south line of Kirby. At
29 the point where the truck stopped, the woman was almost entirely underneath the truck.
30 I definitely heard the thud before I heard the sound of any brakes shrieking. At the time
31 of the thud the front of the truck was about even with the front of my car and was not
32 completely straightened out from making the left turn.
33

34 The sun at the time of the occurrence was extremely bright and low in the sky, coming
35 from a southwesterly direction. I had to shade my eyes when I looked back to the scene
36 after the truck came to a stop.
37

38 After the truck stopped, a man ran out from the car wash across the street, and the
39 driver of the truck got out and went around to the front of the truck. I thought that the
40 guy driving the truck was Charles Shrackle, but I wasn't sure at the time.

1   I stayed at the scene for a couple of minutes, and then I left and went to my appointment
2   with my firm's accountant in the Lincolnshire Shopping Plaza. My appointment was at 3:30
3   p.m. Lincolnshire is about a fifteen minute drive from Kirby and Mattis. I was particularly
4   concerned about the time because traffic had been heavy that day as I came up Mattis.
5   The schools were getting out just as I was traveling on Mattis. What ordinarily would be a
6   ten-minute trip for me took me close to twenty-five minutes.

7

8   I am thirty-seven years old. I work as the office manager of a local construction company,
9   Buildit. Although I don't know Charles Shrackle well, I know his business is a competitor
10 of our company. I have met him at some Builders Association meetings. Frankly, I don't
11 like him much. He has always seemed arrogant—somebody who's always in a hurry to
12 get to the top. It's funny that he is so ambitious, because I don't think his company is
13 doing that well. We took over one school construction job from them a year or so ago
14 when the school district was unhappy with the progress of the work.

15

16 The following morning after I got to work, I read about the accident in the Nita City newspaper.
17 The newspaper article said that the woman was running and was approximately thirty
18 feet south of the crosswalk at the time she was hit by the truck. They got it all wrong. I
19 told my boss, Susannah Bond, about it. Susannah advised me that I should call the police
20 and tell them what I saw. So I called the police and advised them that I had witnessed
21 the accident, and that the woman was in the crosswalk and not running at all.

22

23 Susannah and I then talked about Shrackle some. Susannah told me about Shrackle's
24 problems on the Greenbriar job. She told me there was some possibility we were going
25 to take over that Greenbriar project if Shrackle didn't get his act together.

26

27 I did not know Katherine Potter, nor do I know Jeffrey Potter or anyone else in their family.

28

29 I have read the foregoing and it is a true and accurate transcription of my deposition
30 testimony given on December 12, 2011.

Signed: *Marilyn J. Kelly*   Date: December 12, 2011

Marilyn J. Kelly

Subscribed and sworn to before me this 12th day of December, 2011.

Lucy Madison

Lucy Madison
Notary

SUMMARY OF DEPOSITION OF JUANITA WILLIAMS

1   My name is Juanita Williams. I live at 1010 West Kirby, Unit 15, in Nita City. I work part-time
2   as a secretary. I am a single mother with two children, Victoria, age ten and Joshua, age three.
3
4   On November 30, 2010, at approximately 3:30 p.m. I was at the corner of Kirby and
5   Mattis. I was stopped on Kirby Avenue, west of the intersection, facing east getting
6   ready for the light to change to green. I had just picked up Victoria at Senn School and
7   was driving to pick up Josh at his day care.
8
9   A man in a pickup truck was in the left-hand lane of westbound Kirby on the opposite side of
10 the intersection with his left turn signal on as he was waiting to turn southwest on Mattis.
11 It looked like he was talking on his cell phone or he may have simply had his hand up to his
12 ear. The light changed to green, he waited until I had passed, and with the light still green
13 he turned southwest on Mattis. The pickup truck took the turn a little fast, maybe at about
14 twenty miles an hour. He sort of rolled through the intersection and then picked up speed.
15
16 I actually didn't see him hit the dark-haired woman, who I later found out was Mrs.
17 Potter, but he could not have been going fast because I was only a few feet from the
18 intersection when my daughter said, "Mom, someone was just hit." We immediately
19 turned around and went back to the accident.
20
21 When we went back to the intersection and parked at the White Castle, I saw the dark-haired
22 woman lying underneath the pickup truck. I saw that funny Superman logo on the truck.
23
24 I didn't know Mrs. Potter or anyone in her family. I don't know Charles Shrackle and
25 I never heard of Shrackle Construction Company until the time of the accident.
26
27 I have read the foregoing and it is a true and accurate transcription of my deposition
28 testimony given on December 12, 2011.

Signed: _Juanita Williams_   Date: December 12, 2011

Juanita Williams

Signed and sworn to before me this 12th day of December, 2011.

Joseph Lucey
Notary

SUMMARY OF DEPOSITION OF VICTORIA WILLIAMS

1   My name is Vicky Williams and I am ten years old. I live at 1010 W. Kirby Avenue in Nita
2   City with my mom and my brother, Joshua. Joshua is three.
3
4   My mom was driving me home from school on November 30, 2010. She always picks
5   me up. I was in the back seat in the car. I don't remember if I had my seat belt on but I
6   usually do. I think was about 3:30 in the afternoon when the accident happened.
7
8   We were headed toward town on Kirby Avenue. On the map you showed me that would
9   be going east. (Exhibit 3.) We stopped for a light where Kirby crosses Mattis near the
10 White Castle. There was a man in a truck coming towards us on the opposite side of the
11 intersection getting ready to make a left turn onto Mattis. I was looking at some of my
12 school friends who were on the sidewalk in front of the tire store. There were three or
13 four of them. I waved and smiled at my friends trying to get their attention.
14
15 Then my mom started to move and crossed the intersection. The man in the truck took
16 his turn after we passed him. I saw him because I was looking towards my friends. A lady
17 with black or brown hair, I think, was standing on the center strip on Mattis a little down
18 from the crosswalk. She was facing towards my friends with her back to us. She just
19 stepped right off the center strip right in front of the truck. I saw the truck hit her and
20 her purse went flying into the air. The truck screeched his brakes and stopped. You're
21 right that the sun was a little in my eyes but I could see what happened to the lady. I
22 probably just put my hand up to my forehead so I could see my friends even though the
23 sun was out, but I really don't remember. I know I could see what I told you about.
24
25 I told my mom what happened, that I thought the lady was hit by the truck, and she
26 turned around and we went back and parked in the White Castle parking lot. I saw the
27 lady that got hit lying underneath the truck. It was pretty scary.

Page 14

1.   Q.   Where was the woman when you first saw her?

2.   A.   She was down the crosswalk on Mattis.

3.   Q.   Do you mean south of the crosswalk?

4.   A.   I'm not too good with directions. She was away from Kirby Street.

5.   Q.   How many feet was she away from Kirby?

6.   A.   I'm not too good with guessing feet. I would say maybe twenty feet.

7. Q. Could it have been less?

8. A. Maybe, but I'd say about twenty. Fifteen or twenty.

9. Q. How wide is Mattis Avenue at that point?

10. A. Gee, I don't know. Probably a couple of hundred feet wide.

9 I looked at the map and picture that you called Exhibit 17, and it shows about where
10 we were and what I could see when I first saw the lady standing on the center strip. The
11 map and picture that you called Exhibit 18 shows about where we were when I saw the
12 purse flying in the air.
13
14 I have read the foregoing and it is a true and accurate transcription of my deposition
15 testimony given on December 12, 2011.

Signed: *Victoria Williams*   Date: December 12, 2011

Victoria Williams

Signed and sworn to before me this 12th day of December, 2011.

Joseph Lucey

Joseph Lucey
Notary

SUMMARY OF DEPOSITION OF ALICE MALLORY

1   My name is Alice Mallory. I am forty-seven years old. I am married and have two chil-
2   dren, both of whom are in high school. I work part-time as a school crossing guard at the
3   corner of Mattis and Kirby. I have done that work for about two years. I work both in the
4   morning and in the afternoon at that corner.
5
6   On the afternoon of November 30, 2010, I was working on the southwest corner of the
7   intersection. At about 3:25, I crossed over to the southeast corner of the street by the
8   White Castle to reprimand a small boy who had not heeded my warning to stop. He
9   had run out in front of some cars but luckily wasn't hurt. I was extremely upset by the
10 incident. The boy could have been killed. It would be the worst thing I could imagine—a
11 child being killed while I was the guard. Exhibit 9 shows where I started out in the fore-
12 ground, and also where I was in front of the White Castle when I saw Mrs. Potter across
13 the street. As I knelt to talk to him, I saw over his head a woman, who I later learned was
14 Mrs. Katherine Potter, cross the street from west to east in the crosswalk. I can't remem-
15 ber what she was wearing or much about her, but I remember that she had dark hair.
16
17 When she reached the median, she suddenly turned south and began to walk south on the
18 median strip. I then looked down to continue talking to the boy. I then heard a thump and
19 looked up instantly. I saw Mrs. Potter being carried on the hood of a pickup truck about thirty
20 feet south of the crosswalk. The truck stopped about twenty feet later. I ran over to see if
21 I could help, but others got there before me, so I returned to looking after the children.
22
23 At the time I was watching Mrs. Potter, I was also watching children on the other corner.
24 I was really concerned that one of them would cross the street in a dangerous way. However,
25 I did see clearly all that I have said here. I did not come forward as a witness originally
26 because I was upset and didn't want my story to hurt Mrs. Potter or her family. I was
27 finally contacted by the defendant's lawyer and told her what I saw.
28
29 Three weeks after this incident, just before Christmas, I resigned my position as a school
30 crossing guard. The tension of looking after children was too much for me. I guess I was
31 also affected by Mrs. Potter's accident and death.
32
33 Also, my eyesight has become worse. I have a degenerative eye condition that will get
34 progressively worse as I age. I still see pretty well with corrective lenses and feel that I
35 could have kept on as a guard for a little longer. However, the pressure of concern for the
36 children and the trauma of the accident caused me to quit early.
37
38 Yes, I was wearing my corrective lenses at the time of the accident. My sight is normal
39 with those lenses although there are some limits to my peripheral vision. I have what is
40 known as primary open-angle glaucoma. It was undiagnosed for a long time and hadn't
41 been diagnosed at the time of the accident. They discovered that my central vision
42 is fine, but that I have some weakening peripheral vision. It was just starting to be a

1 problem at the time of the accident. I had surgery about two months ago that my doc-
2 tor says will correct most of the problem.
3
4 I have read the foregoing and it is a true and accurate transcription of my deposition testi-
5 mony given on December 13, 2011.

Signed: _____   Date: December 13, 2011
Alice Mallory

Signed and sworn to before me this 13th day of December, 2011.

Able Ames
Notary

SUMMARY OF DEPOSITION OF BENJAMIN GRIMSON

1   My name is Benjamin Grimson. I just turned nineteen years old. I am presently in prison
2   at Allenwood Prison in Allenwood, Nita.
3
4   On November 30 last year, I was cruising down Mattis in a Camry when I decided to stop for a
5   burger and fries at the White Castle on Kirby. My buddy, Eddie, works there and he waited on
6   me at the drive-through after I placed my order. As I was heading away from the pay booth,
7   I heard a loud thump and when I looked over there was this lady flying in the air on the front
8   of a truck. I yelled, "Holy shit, somebody smashed up that lady." When I saw her she was in
9   mid-air. At that point, I'd say she was about ten feet south of the crosswalk. The truck must
10 have carried her another thirty-five feet or so. When I saw the truck carrying her, it looked like
11 it was still going pretty fast, maybe twenty miles an hour. The truck stopped and the driver
12 got out of the truck. He said something but I couldn't hear what it was. A bunch of people ran
13 over to her. I decided there wasn't anything I could do so I got my burger and drink and got
14 out. There wasn't anybody behind me, so I backed up and went out the Kirby Street entrance.
15
16 The picture that says Exhibit 19 shows the drive-through lane at the White Castle.
17 Exhibits 20 and 21 show what you can see of Mattis Avenue from further down the
18 drive-through lane. That's where I was when I saw this lady.
19
20 Eddie must have told somebody I had been at the drive-through window when the
21 accident occurred. He also told you where to find me.
22
23 On February 25, 2011, I was arrested for grand larceny automobile. I was charged as an
24 adult with the theft of several cars, including the 2008 Toyota Camry I was driving when I
25 saw the accident. The car belonged to one of the teachers at the high school I attended. I am
26 now serving a sentence of two years at Allenwood, which is a minimum security Nita prison.
27
28 I have read the foregoing and it is a true and accurate transcription of my deposition
29 testimony given on December 16, 2011.

Signed: _Benjamin Grimson_   Date: <u>December 16, 2011</u>

Benjamin Grimson

Subscribed and sworn to before me this 16th day of December, 2011.

Tracy Williams

Tracy Williams
Notary

SUMMARY OF DEPOSITION OF MICHAEL YOUNG

1　I am Michael Young. I am a police officer for the Nita Police Department and have been
2　on the police force for seven years. My duties have consisted largely of general patrol
3　duty during that time. I was assigned to patrol duty on November 30, 2010.

4

5　The afternoon of November 30 was clear, the sun was shining. The pavement was dry.
6　There had not been rain for several days. Exhibit 25 is a printout from the Nita City
7　Weather Bureau's Web site that I printed out for that day. I remember later, at the scene
8　of the accident, that I thought that the sun was particularly bright that late fall day. At
9　about 3:30 that afternoon, I was called to the scene of an accident in which a pedestrian
10　had been struck by a vehicle. I was only a few blocks away, on the corner of Greenview
11　and Whitehead Road, and got there within about two minutes. The accident occurred on
12　Mattis Avenue, just south of Kirby. Mattis is a four-lane road at that point with two lanes
13　in either direction. There is a three-foot concrete median separating the north and south-
14　bound lanes. Exhibit 14 is a photo of that median from where it starts at the intersection
15　looking southwest. Exhibit 15 shows the same median looking back up toward Kirby.

16

17　When I arrived at the scene, I found the victim, who I later identified as Katherine Potter, age
18　forty-five, lying underneath a pickup truck. I later identified the driver of the truck as Charles
19　T. Shrackle, age thirty-eight. I asked Mr. Shrackle to move the truck back so that I could have
20　more of an opportunity to provide assistance to Mrs. Potter. He did so. Mrs. Potter was alive
21　and appeared to be conscious. She was moaning and there was a grimace on her face. She
22　appeared to be in a lot of pain. Her eyes were closed for the most part, but she opened them
23　several times. She didn't seem to focus on me or anything else. At one point, it sounded like
24　she said the name "Jeff." She said it maybe three or four times in a row. She didn't say any-
25　thing else. There was no indication of use of alcoholic beverages either by Mrs. Potter or by
26　Mr. Shrackle.

27

28　The photograph, Exhibit 4, is a fair and accurate depiction of Mrs. Potter as she lay on
29　the pavement before the ambulance arrived and after the truck was backed away.

30

31　I waited with Mrs. Potter until the ambulance arrived. After the ambulance took her away,
32　I began in earnest to conduct an investigation. I talked with some other witnesses at the
33　scene, including Jim Marshall and Ed Putnam, who work at the tire store. I also talked to
34　Mr. Shrackle. He told me that he had turned left onto Mattis from Kirby. He said that he
35　felt an impact after he passed the curb south of Kirby Avenue. He remembered that the
36　impact was several seconds after he passed the curb. He didn't know what had happened,
37　but that he took his foot from the accelerator and put it on the brake as hard as he could.
38　He was able to stop the truck and got out and found Mrs. Potter lying underneath it.

39

40　I took measurements of the location of the truck after Mrs. Potter was taken away
41　by the ambulance. The measurements are indicated on my police report. I had Mr.
42　Shrackle move the truck back to the place that it had been, or at least as close as

1 we could figure it was. I measured the distance as fifty-two feet, four inches from the
2 beginning of the crosswalk for pedestrians crossing Mattis on the south side of Kirby.
3 The crosswalk is approximately five feet wide and the limit line on the east side of Mattis
4 is another three feet down from the crosswalk. There were almost seventeen feet of
5 skid marks up to the place where the truck was stopped. These measurements are all
6 on my police accident report, Exhibit 1, which I made as part of my official duties. Based
7 upon the formula that we use, the skid marks would tell us that the truck's minimum
8 speed at the time of the impact would have been thirty-three miles per hour.
9
10 No, I haven't taken the accident reconstruction courses offered by the department yet,
11 but I got the thirty-three miles an hour based on this formula they gave us to help esti-
12 mate speed. No, I don't know whether the formula changes with the type of vehicle. It's
13 just a general formula, I think.
14
15 Based on my investigation, I concluded that no citations were justified. Based on that inves-
16 tigation and my experience, I concluded that Mrs. Potter was out of the crosswalk when she
17 was hit. She was probably fifteen to twenty feet south of the crosswalk at the point of impact.
18
19 The photographs labeled Exhibits 9–21 were taken by me as part of my continuing inves-
20 tigation and at the request of the district attorney's office. They accurately show various
21 views of the intersection of Kirby and Mattis Avenues and environs as they existed on
22 the date of this tragic accident.
23
24 Exhibit 2 is a scale diagram of the intersection of Kirby and Mattis that I obtained from
25 the Nita City Department of Public Works.
26
27 Exhibit 3 is an electronic blow-up of that same intersection showing the various cross-
28 walks and medians. It is to scale. On Exhibits 3a and 3b I placed numbered arrows show-
29 ing where I was standing as I took the photos marked as Exhibits 9–21 and pointing in
30 the direction I was facing as I took each photo.
31
32 I have read the foregoing and it is a true and accurate transcription of my deposition
33 testimony given on October 18, 2011.

Signed: *Michael Young*   Date: October 18, 2011

Michael Young

Subscribed and sworn before me this 18th day of October, 2011.

Harry Gibbons

Harry Gibbons
Notary

SUMMARY OF DEPOSITION OF JAMES MARSHALL

1   I am the owner and operator of Jim Marshall's Tires, 1601 Kirby, Nita City, Nita. I have
2   owned and operated the business for fifteen years. We sell Firestone tires and do state
3   inspections and some kinds of car repair including brakes. We also have a self-wash facility.
4
5   I know Charles Shrackle. He has bought tires from us for both his own car and the vehi-
6   cles used in the construction business. We have also done some inspections and brake
7   work for him. We haven't done any work for them since the accident. Before that time,
8   I'd say he had purchased tires from us a couple of times a year for several years. We had
9   probably inspected all of his cars and trucks.
10
11 I was doing some maintenance work on one of the vacuum units for the car wash at
12 about 3:30 on November 30, 2010. I was standing at the time. It was the second unit
13 from the corner of Mattis. You can see it in the photo marked Exhibit 12, just past the
14 yellow awning. That's my Firestone sign in the background. I saw a dark-haired woman
15 walking east on the south sidewalk of Kirby right in front of my shop.

Page 17

5.   Q. What time was this?

6.   A. About 3:30 in the afternoon.

7.   Q. What did you see?

8.   A. When I first saw the dark-haired woman, she was maybe thirty feet from the

9.   intersection on the sidewalk.

10. Q. What did she look like?

11. A. I remember that she seemed to be in her forties or fifties, but I don't remember

12. what she was wearing or much else about her.

13. Q. Then what happened?

14. A. About a minute or minute and a half later I heard a thump coming from the

15. direction of Mattis Avenue. I ran out to the front of the car wash area and looked toward

16. the spot where I had heard the thud. It was just south of the intersection on Mattis.

17. Q. Can you be more specific as to where that spot was?

18. A. I can't say for sure if the noise came from the area of the crosswalk or was

19. south of it, but it was real close to that point. No more than five feet south

20. of the crosswalk.

21. Q: Just to make sure, how long was it from the time you first saw the woman

22. walking on the sidewalk until you heard the thud?

23. A: No more than a minute, maybe a minute and a half. I had been talking to a

24. customer during that time.

15 Exhibit 13 shows my place across the street and the crosswalk Mrs. Potter headed down,
16 towards where the person taking this picture was standing. The beginning of the cross-
17 walk is shown on the left.
18
19 When I looked in the direction of Mattis, I saw Mr. Shrackle's Toyota pickup carrying a body
20 in front of it. I realized within a few moments that the truck was one we had inspected
21 belonging to the Shrackle Construction Company. You can't miss a Shrackle Construction
22 vehicle with that logo he has on all the doors. I sent one of my employees to see if he
23 could help and called the police on my cell phone. I then went to help and saw that the
24 injured woman was the same woman I had seen walking east on Kirby.
25
26 I stayed near her until the police arrived. I told the police the same thing I just told you.
27 I also told these things to some guy from the insurance company who came to see me a
28 couple of weeks after the accident.
29
30 Exhibit 9 shows the sidewalk outside my business looking east across Mattis towards
31 the White Castle. Mrs. Potter was in the shadow at the bottom of this picture when
32 I first saw her.
33
34 Exhibit 22 is a statement this investigator fellow wrote up after talking to me a couple
35 weeks after the accident. That's my signature at the bottom and initials at the top. He
36 got a couple of things about me wrong. I think he asked me about those things specifi-
37 cally, so I changed them although I didn't really read the statement very carefully. The
38 investigator was in a hurry to get someplace, so I looked it over real quick and signed it.

1 I have read the foregoing and it is a true and accurate transcription of my deposition
2 testimony given on November 27, 2011.

Signed: _James Marshall_   Date: November 27, 2011

         James Marshall

Subscribed and sworn before me this 27th day of November, 2011.

Harry Gibbons

Harry Gibbons
Notary

SUMMARY OF DEPOSITION OF CHARLES T. SHRACKLE

1 I am Charles T. Shrackle, one of the defendants in this case. I live at 1701 West Johnston,
2 Nita City. I am thirty-eight years old.
3
4 I am a self-employed excavating contractor. I started my business, the Shrackle Construction
5 Company, four years ago. Before that time, I worked for various construction firms as a
6 supervisor. Shrackle is a small business corporation. My wife Emily and I are the only
7 stockholders. Our work usually involves digging trenches for dry wells, sewer or water
8 pipes, or for electrical conduits, and installing the pipes or other hardware necessary for
9 the jobs. We then anchor the job, usually with cement, and after the work is checked
10 and approved, refill the excavation. The firm only does excavation work. We do work for
11 developers, for public utilities, and for state and local government. We have twelve full-
12 time employees, and hire a number of laborers each day depending on what work we
13 are doing. We may have as many as fifteen extra people working for us on any given day.
14 Although much of our equipment is rented to fit our needs for particular jobs, we own
15 some, including a backhoe and a couple of dump trucks. We have an excavator and bull-
16 dozer on one-year leases. On November 30, 2010, we were involved in a couple of sewer
17 excavation projects. One was a relatively small one for the city at the corner of John and
18 Holiday Park at the north end of town. The other was a very large project for an extension
19 of the Greenbriar Manor subdivision. Greenbriar Manor is on the south end of town. This
20 project has been giving us some problems. We were past the due date for completion of
21 our portion of the job. It wasn't our fault. We ran into some rock we hadn't expected to
22 find but the general contractor, Clark Poe, was not particularly sympathetic. In fact, Poe
23 had summoned me to a meeting on the afternoon of the accident. He had e-mailed me
24 asking to meet with him, which was a little unusual. Exhibit 23 is that email. We were sup
25 posed to meet at the site at about 3:30. Exhibit 24 is the reply e-mail I sent back to him.
26
27 On the morning of the accident, I got up at 6:45 a.m., my usual time. I had gotten a good
28 night's sleep, probably about seven hours. I was taking no medication and the state of
29 my health was good. I had not had any alcoholic beverages either on the day of the acci-
30 dent or on the day before. I don't use drugs of any kind.
31
32 I started the day at my office, which is in Sommers Township, just at the northeast part
33 of town. I got my crews working by using my cell phone and then went to the John and
34 Holiday Park site. I stayed there most of the day. We were putting the finishing touches
35 on a sewer we had installed. I stayed there until about 2:30 p.m. I then had to make a
36 stop at Nita Builders Supply, which is located near downtown—a couple of miles from
37 the Holiday Park site. I ordered some material there and talked to some of the people
38 in the office. One of the other contractors was talking about how bad business was and
39 how much trouble he was having with some of his subcontractors. He wanted advice
40 on how to cut their charges and how to get them to get their work done on schedule.
41 I was running a little late for my meeting with Poe at Greenbriar, so I cut the conversa-
42 tion short and headed for Greenbriar. I was by myself.

1   Greenbriar is located on South Mattis Street, about five miles from where the
2   accident occurred. I would guess I left Builders Supply about ten after three.

Page 22

11. Q. What did you do once you left Builders Supply?

12. A. I drove down First Street heading out of town. When I got to Kirby

13. I turned right.

14. Q. How long did that take?

15. A. It's about a half mile to Kirby, so I'd say no more than five or ten minutes.

16. Q. Once you turned onto Kirby, what did you do?

17. A. I went straight to Mattis so I could turn and head out to Greenbriar. Mattis is

18. about ten blocks down the way.

19. Q. Did you use your cell phone during this time at all?

20. A. Yes. As I turned onto Kirby I called Poe on my cell phone to tell him I would

21. be a little late.

22. Q. Tell me about that conversation.

23. A. We talked a couple of minutes. Poe told me not to sweat being a little late, but

24. he did say he had an appointment at 4:00 that he would have to leave for so

25. I should get there as soon as I could.

26. Q. Were you still on the phone when you arrived at Mattis?

27. A. I'm not sure. I may have still been talking to him when I got there.

40 The intersection of Mattis and Kirby is about a mile down from
41 where I turned onto Kirby. The light was green. There was moder-
42 ate traffic. I did not come to a complete stop, but slowed for a car
43 that went by before I could make a left turn to go south on Mattis.
44 I started my turn from the southernmost, westbound lane of Kirby. Exhibit 16
45 shows the left-turn lane I was in on the right side of the photograph, and the

1   median I drove around on Mattis on the left side of the photo. Exhibit 11 shows
2   cars making the same turn I made from Kirby onto Mattis.
3
4   I made a gradual turn to the east, southbound lane of Mattis. I observed some school chil-
5   dren, three I think, on the southwest corner of the intersection—where Jim Marshall's car
6   wash is. They were just standing there. I had my eye on them in case one should dart into the
7   path of the car. I didn't know any of the kids and I don't remember much else about them.
8   I think I also observed a crossing guard on the southeast corner of the street. I don't
9   remember any other pedestrians.
10
11 I remember making the turn and there was the impact and that was it. The impact took
12 place several seconds after I passed south of the Kirby Avenue sidewalk. I was probably
13 about four feet west of the median.
14
15 I did not see Mrs. Potter before the impact. I did not apply my brakes before the impact,
16 although as I made the turn I had my foot on the brake pedal. I usually make my left turns
17 that way. I was probably traveling about fifteen miles an hour at the time of the impact.
18
19 I remember that it was a clear day and that the sun was out. It bothered me a little as
20 I was making the turn because Mattis at that point goes southwest and at that time of
21 day the sun was pretty low in the sky. I could still see in front of me. I had my eye on the
22 children on the corner all the time.
23
24 I both heard and felt the impact, but I didn't immediately know what I had hit. The
25 impact was on the left front of my vehicle. As soon as I felt the impact, I applied the
26 brakes with as much force as I could. As I said, my foot was already on the brake. The
27 vehicle stopped quickly and I jumped out. I moved around the front of the car and I saw
28 Mrs. Potter lying under it. She was lying almost straight, with her head under the front
29 bumper and her feet straight back. Her head was pointed south and her feet north. She
30 seemed to be conscious, and I asked her, "Where did you come from?" She didn't reply.
31
32 The police arrived almost immediately. We got a first aid kit out of my truck and applied
33 a compress to her forehead and we waited for the ambulance to come. There were skid
34 marks and the police measured them. There was a mark on the left-hand side of the
35 hood of my truck, near the division between the hood and the fender.
36
37 At the time of the accident I was driving a 2001 Toyota Tacoma truck. My truck was in
38 good condition at the time of the accident. I had had the car inspected and the brakes
39 checked about a month before the accident. As a matter of fact, Jim Marshall did the
40 inspection. The tires were relatively new. I think they had less than 5,000 miles on them.
41 Exhibit 6 shows me and my truck at a job site out in Ferndale just after I got it. That's the
42 kind of cell phone I use, the hand-held kind. The logo shown on the truck in that exhibit,
43 and more closely in Exhibit 7, is my company logo.

1 At the time of the accident, I was covered by an automobile liability policy of $500,000 per
2 person and $1 million per accident. The policy was with Boston Casualty. The policy num-
3 ber is FA606560, effective September 23, 2010 to September 23, 2011. Except for the fact
4 that there is concern that this action will exceed the policy limits, the insurance company
5 hasn't indicated any problem with my coverage. I also have a $5 million umbrella policy
6 for the company with Boston Casualty. They have also been notified about this accident.
7
8 I did not meet with Clark Poe at Greenbriar that day. Shortly after they took Mrs. Potter
9 away in the ambulance, I called him on my cell phone and told him what had happened.
10 We met the next day. Based on our conversation, there was a reduction in the amount
11 we were to be paid for the job. I wasn't too happy about the result, but compared to
12 Mrs. Potter's situation it was no big deal.
13
14 Ordinarily it would take me about twenty minutes to get from Builders Supply to
15 Greenbrier. However, it could take longer on weekday afternoons about that time
16 because of the schools getting out. The traffic was a little heavy before I got to the inter-
17 section of Kirby and Mattis, but not too bad. I thought that it might get worse after I
18 turned on Mattis, particularly down about a mile when the road narrows. It's highway at
19 that point, but two lanes. But I felt I'd make it in plenty of time for my meeting with Poe.
20
21 I have read the foregoing and it is a true and accurate transcription of my deposition
22 testimony given on December 16, 2011.

Signed: *Charles T. Shrackle*　　　　　　　　　　　　Date: December 16, 2011

Charles T. Shrackle

Subscribed and sworn before me this 16th day of December, 2011.

Terry Anderson

Terry Anderson
Notary

SUMMARY OF DEPOSITION OF JEFFREY POTTER

1   I am Jeffrey Potter, the plaintiff in this case, and I live at 4920 Thorndale in Nita City in

2   the same house that Katherine and I lived in before her death. I am forty-nine years of

3   age. I'm a professor in the physics department at the University of Nita. I received a

4   bachelor's degree in physics from Purdue and a doctorate in physics from the University

5   of Wisconsin/Madison. I received my PhD twenty-four years ago and have been at the

6   University of Nita since 1983.

7

8   Katherine and I were married twelve years ago, June 15, 1999. We met because we sang

9   in the same community chorus. She was a high school computer science teacher then.

10   She got a BS in computer science from Nita City University in 1986. She worked on her

11   PhD in computer science from 1986 to 1988, but never finished. She had done all of

12   her course work, but had not completed her dissertation. She told me she decided that

13   she could accomplish more for herself and the world by teaching in high school and she

14   didn't need a PhD to do that. But, by the time we met in 1998, she was disillusioned

15   with teaching. She was tired of working as hard as you do as a high school teacher and

16   not making much money.

[handwritten margin note: who she was]

17

18   Shortly after we got married she left teaching and began working for Techno-Soft, Inc.,

19   a software company. She loved the work at Techno-Soft and was making a great deal

20   more money. She became very ambitious in her work situation, but not so much that

21   we didn't have a good time together. I was busy with my work as well, so our schedule

22   and career goals were compatible.

23

24   Despite both of our involvement in our work, Katherine and I had other interests and

25   spent a great deal of time together. We would go to movies and out to dinner whenever

26   we could. We also liked to sing and we stayed with the community chorus. She had a

27   beautiful alto voice; I am a so-so bass. We would almost always make the practices,

28   which were once a week. There were concerts about four times a year and we would

29   rehearse even more frequently as we got closer to concert time.

30

31   We also loved to travel, particularly to Europe. I had the summers free and we would

32   take every three-week vacation that Katherine had to travel. Tuscany and Umbria were

33   our favorites. We loved to walk in the Italian countryside or have a glass of wine or cof-

34   fee at a sidewalk café. We had a pretty special relationship until Shrackle took her life. I

35   think we had about as near perfect a relationship as is possible in a marriage.

36

37   I did write the letter to Dr. Stevens marked Exhibit 28. As I said in the letter, I thought our

38   marriage would work out just fine. Kathy and I, like most couples, had some difficulties

39   over the years. She was always driven by her work, both teaching and with Techno-Soft,

40   and that was an ongoing problem. We also disagreed ultimately about having children.

41   We tried to achieve a pregnancy early on in our marriage and had difficulties. After a lot

42   of testing, the doctors couldn't identify a problem, but we still never conceived. I wanted

1 to explore in vitro fertilization and/or adoption, but Kathy was ultimately opposed and
2 we resigned ourselves to our very comfortable life.
3
4 Around the time of Kathy's death, we were having a disagreement over retirement. I
5 wanted Kathy to take an early retirement so we could travel more, and she wanted to
6 continue working. She was very <u>ambitious</u>. We were working through that problem with
7 Dr. Stevens at the time that Kathy was killed. Although it was a bone of contention it did
8 not threaten our marriage. Although I said in the letter that I might seek another rela-
9 tionship if our marriage didn't work out, that was a remote possibility. We had always
10 been able to work out our problems, whatever they were. No, I did not have another
11 relationship in mind at that time or at any time during our marriage, and I resent your
12 insinuation. I was completely faithful to Kathy and she to me. After Kathy died, I saw Dr.
13 Stevens briefly, maybe three times, and he helped me with my grieving, but ultimately
14 you have to learn to live with your loss and time is the best healer.
15
16 Katherine had done well at Techno-Soft and they seemed to like her. Although times are
17 tough in the software business, Techno-Soft has done fairly well.

Page 18

14. Q. How did Katherine like her work?

15. A. Techno-soft gave her very interesting work projects, although she had to work

16. long hours, and she certainly enjoyed making some real money after all those

17. years in teaching.

18. Q. How did you feel about her work?

19. A. I liked the fact she found her work rewarding, but I thought she might want to take

20. it easy and spend more time traveling.

21. Q. Had you talked to her about the possibility of retiring?

22. A. I had talked to her now and again about retiring and traveling with me during the

23. summers. She seemed to be interested in the idea, but hadn't agreed to it. I

24. suggested to her that those years might be better spent enjoying herself traveling.

43 We had a 50-50 partnership marriage. All of our income was pooled and we shared
44 household chores equally. We shared all of the things that have to be done to maintain
45 a home and a relationship. I did most of the cooking and shopping for food. Kathy did

1   most of the laundry and cleaning. We liked to do gardening together and split those
2   chores. I did most of the repair work around the house like minor electrical or plumb-
3   ing problems, but Kathy was the better painter and when the house needed inside
4   painting, Kathy did that. Kathy was in charge of the finances. She did the bills each
5   month, wrote out checks on the computer. She also did the banking and the taxes.
6   Although we talked about the investments we made, Kathy was really more inter-
7   ested and knew more about the stock market. I followed her advice in allocating my
8   University retirement account among different mutual funds. She was very good at that.
9   I was the one who planned our travel. I liked to do that and had more time than Kathy in
10 light of everything else she did plus her job, which was demanding.
11
12 I will never forget hearing about Katherine's accident—if you can call that kind of reckless-
13 ness on Shrackle's part an accident. I was in my office talking to one of my students, Cheryl
14 Tobias, when the departmental secretary knocked on the door and told me that Katherine
15 had been in a serious accident. I rushed over to the hospital, Nita Memorial, and found her
16 in the emergency room. She was unconscious when I first saw her. Later, in the intensive
17 care unit, her eyes would open from time to time but she never said anything. She would
18 generally moan softly during both her waking moments and even when she seemed to
19 be unconscious. She appeared to be in considerable pain the whole time in the hospital.
20
21 I stayed at the hospital during the days before her death. Friends brought me clean
22 clothes and I was able to shower there. Those were the longest four days of my life. Even
23 when the doctors were pessimistic, I was hopeful for a miracle, but it just didn't hap-
24 pen. When she died, I just went back to the empty house. It took me six months before
25 I could begin to clear out some of her clothes, books, and papers. I still haven't cleared
26 it all out. I can't believe what has happened to me since Kathy's death. I sit at home day
27 after day, watching television or listening to music. I can't even read a book. I seldom go
28 out, except to teach my classes. I am sure that my teaching has suffered. Certainly, I no
29 longer have the close working relationship with my students that I had when Kathy was
30 alive. I'm alone all the time and I'm lonely.

How Death effected him

31
32 Our house is located two blocks down from Greenview Avenue on the east side of
33 the street. I assume Kathy was walking home at the time she was struck down by Mr.
34 Shrackle. Kathy and I loved to walk through Senn Park. There were times we would walk
35 through the park rather than walking all the way down Thorndale from Kirby just to
36 enjoy the beauty of the park.
37
38 Exhibit 5 is a fair and accurate depiction of Katherine as she looked before the accident.
39 The photograph was taken in our backyard about a year before her death.
40
41 Yes, as I mentioned, I do know a young woman named Cheryl Tobias. She was and
42 is a graduate student at the University, and she had just completed a class with me
43 as a teaching assistant in the fall semester of 2010 when Kathy died. I believe I said
44 that she was actually in my office when I got the news about Kathy's injuries. Yes,
45 she and I have developed a personal relationship since Kathy's death. I have not

• relationship
• effect of death

1 supervised any of her work since the fall 2010 semester. That would be improper given
2 our personal relationship. Despite our age difference, she's twenty-four, we have a lot
3 in common and Cheryl shares my interest in traveling. Yes, Exhibits 29 and 30 are travel
4 records from a trip we took together to Martinique and Exhibit 30 is a copy of our bill
5 from that same trip. Exhibit 32 is a photo of Cheryl and me. Our relationship is develop-
6 ing slowly. We have been intimate but Cheryl has not moved in with me, or me with her,
7 and we have no plans to do so. I can't say what will happen in the future. Our age differ-
8 ence doesn't bother Cheryl, but I'm concerned it will become a problem in the future.
9 Also, she has her whole career ahead of her. She's very bright and I don't know how that
10 will jibe with my work plans in the future. Although I value my relationship with Cheryl
11 and she's helped me deal with Kathy's death, she'll never take Kathy's place in my heart,
12 and I doubt my relationship with Cheryl will ever be as fulfilling as what I had with Kathy.
13 We were soul mates and I think that only happens once in your life if you're lucky.
14
15 Yes, I still live in the same house Kathy and I bought together.
16
17 Exhibit 26 is the bill from Nita Memorial Hospital, which has been paid. Exhibit 27 is the
18 invoice from the funeral home, which also has been paid.
19
20 I have read the foregoing and it is a true and accurate transcription of my deposition
21 testimony given November 28, 2011, *year since accident*

Signed: *Jeffrey T. Potter*   Date: <u>November 28, 2011</u>

Jeffrey Potter

Subscribed and sworn before me this 28th day of November, 2011.

Harry Gibbons

Harry Gibbons,
Notary

Summary of Deposition of Daniel Sloan

1   I am forty-eight years old. I am the principal shareholder and chief executive officer of
2   Techno-Soft, Inc. We are a small company with about fifty employees. We provide soft-
3   ware for various high-tech manufacturing companies. The software we have developed
4   is used in delicate manufacturing processes in the electronics industry.
5
6   Katherine Potter started working for us in 1999. Her starting salary was $34,000 a year.
7   Her salary increased on an annual basis until, in 2010, she was making a base salary
8   of $85,000 in the position of Technology Training Specialist. At the time of her death,
9   her fringe benefits package was twenty percent of her salary. This included contribu-
10   tion to the retirement plan, medical, and dental insurance, as well as life and disability
11   insurance. As an example of what we thought of her, we gave her a bonus of $2,000 in
12   January, 2010. The bonus was, in part, simply a recognition of her value to the company
13   but it was also in recognition of the fact that she had spent more than ten years with us.
14   Through our human resources director, Linda Graham, I provided all of the details of her
15   employment to Robert Glenn, the economist working for Mr. Potter's lawyer.
16
17   Katherine was one of our prize employees. She had consistently received raises at the
18   highest level of all employees. I fully expected her to continue that pattern. She was
19   smart and worked very hard. She also was very ambitious. She kept talking about all
20   those years she spent working for peanuts as a high school teacher. In fact, I was groom-
21   ing her to become an executive vice-president, she was that good. No, it wasn't cer-
22   tain that she would be made a vice-president. If she did receive that promotion, and
23   in my opinion there was a good chance she would have, it likely would have occurred
24   in three or so years, by about 2014 or 2015. The current salary range for that position
25   is $120,000–$150,000 a year. Also, people at that level typically receive bonuses in the
26   $10,000 range based on good performance. Our business is expanding and Katherine
27   was exactly the kind of person we needed. She had all of the technical skills as well as an
28   extraordinary ability to work with people.
29
30   Katherine did tell me that her husband, Jeffrey, was always after her to retire early. He's
31   a college professor and has the summers off. They both loved to travel. Katherine told
32   me that this was a dream of Jeff's and she had told him that she would think about it.   } relationship
33   She told me that there was no way that she would retire before she was sixty. She told
34   me that she loved her job and that all of the things she did with Jeff were okay, but work
35   was really her first love. I am absolutely confident she would have stayed on.
36
37   Even in the very remote possibility that she would have left her current duties, she could   } use this
38   have gone part-time. A number of our employees in their fifties have done that and, given
39   the nature of our work, we can accommodate them by permitting them to work at home.
40
41   We'll sure miss Katherine. I hope that Jeffrey gets through all of this in one piece. I've
42   always seen him as a pretty fragile guy.

1   I have read the foregoing and it is a true and accurate transcription of my deposition
2   testimony given November 29, 2011.

Signed: *Daniel Sloan*   Date: November 29, 2011

Daniel Sloan

Subscribed and sworn before me this 29th day of November, 2011.

Harry Gibbons

Harry Gibbons
Notary

Expert Report of
Robert Glenn, PhD
Professor of Economics
University of Nita

State of Nita Circuit Court
Circuit Court of Darrow County
Civil Division

Jeffrey T. Potter, the Administrator of the Estate of Katherine Potter,
and Jeffrey T. Potter, individually
(Plaintiff)
v.
Charles T. Shrackle and The Shrackle Construction Company
(Defendants)

Dated: July 1, 2011

Introduction

I, Robert Glenn, understand this matter involves Jeffrey T. Potter, the Administrator of the Estate of Katherine Potter, and Jeffrey T. Potter, individually, as plaintiff, and Charles T. Shrackle and The Shrackle Construction Company (collectively, "Shrackle") as defendants. As I understand this matter, Ms. Katherine Potter was struck by an automobile driven by Mr. Charles T. Shrackle on November 30, 2010. Ms. Potter died on December 4, 2010 as a result of injuries sustained in that accident.

Engagement of Robert Glenn

As part of this engagement, Madden & James, counsel for plaintiffs, requested that I:

1. Review the Potter v. Shrackle case file, including but not limited to:
   a. the complaint and answer;
   b. statements of Marilyn J. Kelly, Juanita Williams, Victoria Williams, Alice Mallory, and Benjamin Grimson;
   c. depositions of James Marshall, Victoria Williams, Michael Young, Charles T. Shrackle, Jeffrey Potter, and Daniel Sloan; and
   d. other documents provided by counsel;
2. Collect information relevant to a calculation of economic losses resulting from a wrongful death; and
3. Provide economic and statistical analysis regarding plaintiff's specific claims.

In preparing my analysis, I have relied on counsel, Madden & James, for any interpretation of legal issues.

Supplemental Analysis and Opinions

I understand that discovery in this matter is still ongoing and that additional documents, statements, depositions, or trial testimony on topics relevant to the opinions issued in this report may be forthcoming. As a result, I reserve the right to supplement this report or to address any such testimony at trial.

Opinion

Based upon my continuing review and analysis of the Potter v. Shrackle case file, supplemented with my own research of relevant economic and demographic information, I have developed the following opinion regarding economic damages in this matter.

1. From the date of her death through her eventual retirement at age 60, the value of Katherine Potter's lost earnings, benefits and household work, and net of her consumption is a loss of $2,334,579 to her estate and to her husband, Jeffrey Potter. In present discounted value, this amount is a loss of $1,532,021 to the plaintiff.

Bases for Opinions

1. Katherine Potter was in good health at the time of her death and would have reasonably been expected to work until at least the age of 60 before her retirement.
2. Katherine Potter was happy with her position as a Technology Training Specialist at Techno-Soft, Inc. I believe the pattern of her salary growth from the date of her death

to her eventual retirement at age 60 would be similar to the average pattern of salary growth during her period of employment with the company.

3. Katherine Potter would have continued to enjoy her fringe benefits as an employee of Techno-Soft, Inc. I have spoken with Ms. Linda Graham, Human Resources Director at Techno-Soft, Inc. and have learned that Katherine Potter's benefits amounted to 20 percent of her income at the time of her death.

4. Katherine Potter shared equally in the household work with her husband, Jeffrey Potter, and her death will result in a loss equal to the value of Katherine's labor, which equaled approximately $41 per hour at the date of her death.

Exhibits

For purposes of presenting our opinions and their bases, I may develop and use exhibits including overheads, flip charts, and other summary graphics. I may also use certain demonstrative aids and illustrations in presenting technical concepts and analyses.

Compensation

The hourly rates for myself and my research associates who worked on this matter range between $75 and $350 per hour. My hourly rate is $350 per hour.

Qualifications

I am a Professor of Economics at the University of Nita in Nita City with fields of concentration in labor economics and microeconomics. I hold a bachelors degree in economics from the University of North Carolina (1994) and a PhD in economics from the University of Illinois (1998). I have taught economics at the undergraduate and graduate level at the University of Nita for fourteen years as well as numerous seminars in the industry. As part of my duties as a professor at a research institution, I direct graduate research, conduct independent research, and publish my results in academic economic journals. In addition to my publications, I have received research grants from the National Science Foundation, the Social Science Research Council, the Center for Comparative Studies at the University of Nita, and the Nita Law Enforcement Commission.

February 1, 2012

Robert Glenn
Professor of Economics, University of Nita

POTTER v. SHRACKLE AND THE SHRACKLE CONSTRUCTION COMPANY DAMAGES MODEL OF ROBERT GLENN, PH.D.

TABLE 1. SUMMARY OF ECONOMIC LOSS, WRONGFUL DEATH OF KATHERINE POTTER

Summary of Economic Loss

		NominalDollars	Present DiscountedValue
A.	Future Value of Earnings	$2,918,363	$1,915,118
B.	Future Value of Fringe Benefits	$583,673	$383,024
c.	Future Value of Household Work	$1,024,233	$672,133
D.	Future Value of Personal Consumption	$2,191,691	$1,438,254
E.	Total Value of Loss (A+B+C-D)	$2,334,579	$1,532,021

POTTER v. SHRACKLE AND THE SHRACKLE CONSTRUCTION COMPANY
DAMAGES MODEL OF ROBERT GLENN, PHD

TABLE 2. FUTURE VALUE OF EARNINGS OF KATHERINE POTTER AGE 45 TO 60

Date of Birth:	June 15, 1965
Date of Death:	December 4, 2010
Appraisal Period:	2010 – 2025
Projected Retirement Age:	60
Discount Rate:	6.00%
Earnings Growth Rate:	9.80%

Year	Projected Age	Projected Value Earnings	Present Discounted Value of Earnings
2010	45	$85,000	
2011	46	$93,329	$93,329
2012	47	$102,474	$102,474
2013	48	$112,515	$106,146
2014	49	$123,540	$109,950
2015	50	$135,645	$113,890
2016	51	$148,936	$117,971
2017	52	$163,530	$122,199
2018	53	$179,554	$126,578
2019	54	$197,147	$131,114
2020	55	$216,465	$135,813
2021	56	$237,676	$140,680
2022	57	$260,965	$145,721
2023	58	$286,536	$150,943
2024	59	$314,612	$156,353
2025	60	$345,440	$161,956
	Value of Future Earnings:	$2,918363	$1,915,118

POTTER v. SHRACKLE AND THE SHRACKLE CONSTRUCTION COMPANY
DAMAGES MODEL OF ROBERT GLENN, PHD

TABLE 3. HISTORICAL EARNINGS GROWTH OF KATHERINE POTTER, 1987 TO 2010

Date of Birth: June 15, 1965
Date of Death: December 4, 2010
Observation Period: 1987 to 2010

2010
− 1965
(45)

Year	Age	Earnings	%Change from Previous Year	Job
1987to1989	22-24	$0	n/a	(1)
1990	25	$19,000	n/a	(2)
1991	26	$19,600	3.2%	(2)
1992	27	$20,250	3.3%	(2)
1993	28	$20,900	3.2%	(2)
1994	29	$21,600	3.3%	(2)
1995	30	$22,300	3.2%	(2)
1996	31	$23,000	3.1%	(2)
1997	32	$23,750	3.3%	(2)
1998	33	$24,500	3.2%	(2)
1999	34	$25,400	3.7%	(2)/(3)
2000	35	$34,000	33.9%	(3)
2001	36	$42,000	23.5%	(3)
2002	37	$50,000	19.0%	(3)
2003	38	$57,500	15.0%	(3)
2004	39	$62,500	8.7%	(3)
2005	40	$67,500	8.0%	(3)
2006	41	$71,000	5.2%	(3)
2007	42	$73,500	3.5%	(3)
2008	43	$76,000	3.4%	(3)
2009	44	$78,000	2.6%	(3)
2010	45	$85,000	9.0%	(3)
2011	Deceased	$0	100.0%	Deceased

Average Income Growth Rate (2000 to 2010): 9.80%

Job Information:

(1) Attending Graduate School, University of Nita
(2) Computer Instructor, Nita City Unified School District
(3) Computer Instructor, Techno-Soft, Inc.

**POTTER v. SHRACKLE AND THE SHRACKLE CONSTRUCTION
COMPANY DAMAGES MODEL OF ROBERT GLENN, PHD**

TABLE 4. FUTURE VALUE OF FRINGE BENEFITS OF KATHERINE POTTER, AGE 45 TO 60

Date of Birth:	June 15, 1965
Date of Death:	December 4, 2010
Appraisal Period:	2011 to 2025
Projected Retirement Age:	60
Discount Rate:	6.00%
Benefits as % of Income:	20.00%

Year	*ProjectedAge*	*ProjectedValue ofFringe Benefits*	*Present Discounted ValueofFringe Benefits*
2010	45	$17,000	
2011	46	$18,666	$18,666
2012	47	$20,495	$20,495
2013	48	$22,503	$21,229
2014	49	$24,708	$21,990
2015	50	$27,129	$22,778
2016	51	$29,787	$23,594
2017	52	$32,706	$24,440
2018	53	$35,911	$25,316
2019	54	$39,429	$26,223
2020	55	$43,293	$27,163
2021	56	$47,535	$28,136
2022	57	$52,193	$29,144
2023	58	$57,307	$30,189
2024	59	$62,922	$31,271
2025	60	$69,088	$32,391
Value of Future Fringe Benefits:		$583,673	$383,024

POTTER v. SHRACKLE AND THE SHRACKLE CONSTRUCTION COMPANY
DAMAGES MODEL OF ROBERT GLENN, PHD

TABLE 5. FUTURE VALUE OF HOUSEHOLD WORK OF KATHERINE POTTER, AGE 45 TO 60

Date of Birth:	June 15, 1965
Date of Death:	December 4, 2010
Appraisal Period:	2011 to 2025
Projected Retirement Age:	60
Discount Rate:	6.00%
# of Hours Per Day at Household Work:	2
Days Per Year Doing Household Work:	365

Year	Projected Age	Projected Value of Household Work	Present Discounted Value of Household Work
2010	45	$29,832	
2011	46	$32,755	$32,755
2012	47	$35,964	$35,964
2013	48	$39,488	$37,253
2014	49	$43,358	$38,588
2015	50	$47,606	$39,971
2016	51	$52,271	$41,403
2017	52	$57,393	$42,887
2018	53	$63,016	$44,424
2019	54	$69,191	$46,016
2020	55	$75,971	$47,665
2021	56	$83,415	$49,373
2022	57	$91,589	$51,143
2023	58	$100,563	$52,975
2024	59	$110,417	$54,874
2025	60	$121,236	$56,840
Value of Future Household Work:		$1,024,233	$672,133

Assumption:

(1)   There are 2,080 work hours in a year (52 weeks* 40 hours per week)

POTTER v. SHRACKLE AND THE SHRACKLE CONSTRUCTION COMPANY
DAMAGES MODEL OF ROBERT GLENN, PHD

TABLE 6. FUTURE VALUE OF PERSONAL CONSUMPTION OF KATHERINE POTTER, AGE 45 TO 60

Date of Birth:	June 15, 1965
Date of Death:	December 4, 2010
Appraisal Period:	2011 to 2025
Projected Retirement Age:	60
Discount Rate:	6.00%
Consumption as % of Income:	75.10%

Year	Projected Age	Projected Value of Personal Consumption	Present Discounted Value of Personal Consumption
2010	45	$63,835	
2011	46	$70,090	$70,090
2012	47	$76,958	$76,958
2013	48	$84,499	$79,716
2014	49	$92,778	$82,572
2015	50	$101,869	$85,531
2016	51	$111,851	$88,597
2017	52	$122,811	$91,772
2018	53	$134,845	$95,060
2019	54	$148,058	$98,467
2020	55	$162,565	$101,996
2021	56	$178,495	$105,651
2022	57	$195,985	$109,437
2023	58	$215,188	$113,359
2024	59	$236,274	$117,421
2025	60	$259,425	$121,629
Value of Future Consumption:		$2,191,691	$1,438,254

TABLE 6. FUTURE VALUE OF PERSONAL CONSUMPTION OF KATHERINE POTTER,
AGE 45 TO 60

TABLE 6 NOTES

(1) To arrive at Katherine Potter's net contribution to the Potter household welfare (i.e. what Jeffrey Potter will lose monetarily as a result of his wife's death), the future value of Katherine's consumption expenditures should be subtracted from the future value of her income, fringe benefits, and household work.

(2) The U.S. Department of Labor has calculated that, on average, household expenditures amount to 89.1% of household income for American households.

(3) Of this amount, on average, 28% of household income is spent on housing expenses.

(4) In this matter, half of this amount should be excluded from Katherine Potter's share of income spent on household expenses since housing is a benefit equally shared by both Katherine and Jeffrey Potter. Katherine's death is a loss to Mr. Potter insofar as Katherine contributed to the cost of housing for their household.

(5) As a result, 75.1% of Katherine's future wage and salary earnings should be subtracted from her total wage and salary earnings to account for the value of her expenditures.

Source:

> U.S. Department of Labor, Bureau of Labor Statistics, Consumer Expenditures in 2008, May 2010, Report 949, Table 2.

Future Value of Income
Fringe Benefits
+ Household Work
─────────────────
− Consumption exp.
─────────────────
= net contribution

Robert Glenn, PhD
Goldman Sachs Professor of Economics
University of Nita, Department of Economics, Campus Locator #43
Nita City, Nita
(555) 444-2308, Fax (555) 444-2307
glennecon@email.nita.edu

Education

BS University of North Carolina (1992) (economics)
PhD University of Illinois (1997) (economics)

Employment History

Assistant Professor, University of Nita, 1997-2003
Associate Professor, University of Nita 2003-2007
Professor, University of Nita, 2008-2011
Goldman Sachs Professor, 2011-

Principal publications since 2001:

Books
Microeconomics in a Time of Terrorism, Oxford University Press (2011)

Loss Evaluation in Wrongful Death Cases, Aspen (2009)

Articles
"The Effect of September 11 on Microeconomic Theory," 80 Harvard Public Policy Review 1769 (2011)

"Is Your Loss Worth Anything?" 5 Journal of Law and Economics 1289 (2009)

"Can Our Economic System Survive a Terrorist Attack?" 45 Economics and Politics 549 (2008)

"Valuing Services and Potential Retirement," 19 Journal of Labor Economics 42 (2004)

Sample Expert Testimony

(I have been qualified as an expert in economics in 24 different cases. I have testified for the plaintiff in all but 3 cases.)

Michaels v. Hammer, North Carolina Superior Court, October 2011 (personal injury, testified for plaintiff)

Smith v. Tucker, United States District Court (SDNY) (personal injury, testified for plaintiff)

Rosen v. Nichol, United States District Court (S. D. Calif.) (wrongful death, testified for plaintiff)

Glandon v. Schwartz, Nita Superior Court, May, 2008 (wrongful death case, testified for plaintiff)

State of Nita Circuit Court Circuit Court of Darrow
County Civil Division

Jeffrey T. Potter, the Administrator of the Estate
of Katherine Potter, and Jeffrey T. Potter,
individually
(Plaintiff)

v.

Charles T. Shrackle and
The Shrackle Construction Company
(Defendants)

Expert Report of Elizabeth Buchanan, PhD Assistant
Professor of Economics, Nita State University
Nita City, Nita

September 1, 2011

1.0 Introduction

I, Elizabeth C. Buchanan, PhD, understand this matter involves Jeffrey T. Potter, the Administrator of the Estate of Katherine Potter, and Jeffrey T. Potter, individually, as plaintiff, and Charles T. Shrackle and The Shrackle Construction Company (collectively, "Shrackle") as defendants. As I understand this matter, Ms. Katherine Potter was struck by an automobile driven by Mr. Charles T. Shrackle on November 30, 2010. Ms. Potter died on December 4, 2010, as a result of injuries sustained in that accident.

2.0 Qualifications

I am an Assistant Professor of Economics at Nita State University with fields of concentration in labor economics and industrial organization. I am also a graduate of the University of Nita, holding both a bachelors and doctorate degree in economics. I have taught at Nita State University for the past five years: two years as a visiting professor, two years as a lecturer, and one year as an assistant professor. Appendix A is a copy of my current resume. It contains a listing of my papers and publications for the past ten years.

2.1 Engagement of Elizabeth Buchanan

As part of this engagement, James Barber of Pierce, Johnson & Clark ("Pierce"), counsel for defendants Shrackle, requested that I:

- Review the expert report on damages prepared by Dr. Robert Glenn;

- Review the Potter v. Shrackle case file, including but not limited to:
  - the complaint and answer;
  - depositions of James Marshall, Victoria Williams, Michael Young, Charles T. Shrackle, Jeffrey Potter, and Daniel Sloan;
  - statements of Marilyn J. Kelly, Juanita Williams, Victoria Williams, Alice Mallory, Benjamin Grimson; and
  - other documents which I have reviewed which have been produced in this matter;

- Collect information relevant to a calculation of economic losses resulting from a wrongful death; and

- Provide economic and statistical analysis regarding plaintiff's specific claims.

In preparing my analysis, I have relied on counsel, Pierce, for any interpretation of legal issues.

2.2 Supplemental Analysis and Opinions

I understand that discovery in this matter is still ongoing and that additional documents, statements, deposition, or trial testimony on topics relevant to the opinions issued in this report may be forthcoming. As a result, I reserve the right to supplement this report or to address any such testimony at trial.

3.0 Opinion

Based upon my continuing review and analysis of Dr. Glenn's expert report and the Potter v. Shrackle case file, supplemented with my own research of relevant economic and demographic information, I have developed the following opinion regarding economic damages in this matter.

- Dr. Robert Glenn substantially overstates the total value of loss allegedly suffered by the plaintiff due to incorrect and inappropriate assumptions used in his damages model.

- In my own opinion, from the date of her death through her eventual retirement at age 55, the value of Katherine Potter's lost earnings, benefits and household work, net of her consumption is a loss of $411,077 to her estate and to her husband, Jeffrey Potter. In present discounted value, this amount is a loss of $333,719 to the plaintiff.

4.0 Bases for Opinions

- It is my opinion that Katherine Potter would have reasonably been expected to work full-time until the age of 50 and then would work part-time until her retirement at age 55. Deposition testimony from her husband, Jeffrey Potter, stated that he and Katherine talked about taking an early retirement. My calculations of loss valuation is conservative in that it treats Katherine as having worked to the age of 55, which would tend to overstate the loss if she were to retire before that age.

- It is my opinion that Katherine Potter would have an average annual salary increase of five percent per year. Dr. Glenn averages Katherine's salary increases during her entire period of employment at Techno-Soft, Inc. This method would overstate the salary increases Katherine would likely receive in the period after her death. I note that her salary increases are smaller and smaller, in percentage terms, and thus the use of long-run averages would be ignorant of this trend. Instead, I use an average of her annual salary increases over the last three years to capture the fact that she may be reaching the upper salary limit of her position.

- I assume that the imputed value of benefits enjoyed by Katherine Potter is 17.5 percent of her annual salary. Like Dr. Glenn, I have spoken to Linda Graham, Human Resources Director at Techno-Soft, Inc. Based upon my discussion with Ms. Graham, I learned that Dr. Glenn's calculation of future fringe benefits overstates this value since it ignores the fact that Katherine Potter received a special one-time bonus payout of $2,000 in 2010 for staying beyond ten years at Techno-Soft, Inc. Were this one-time payout to be removed, the actual rate of benefits would be lowered from 20% to 17.5% of her annual salary. Dr. Glenn thus overstates all future projections for fringe benefit calculations since he does not appropriately evaluate the baseline year. I use the more justifiable number of 17.5 percent in my projections.

- Although Katherine Potter shared equally in the household work with her husband, Jeffrey Potter, and her death will result in a loss equal to the value of Katherine's labor, I disagree with Dr. Glenn's methodology of using her imputed hourly wage as the appropriate replacement wage. Katherine's hourly wage, assuming a 2,080-hour work year, is imputed to be approximately $41 per hour. Dr. Glenn uses this amount as the value of Katherine's lost labor. This methodology is incorrect in that Dr. Glenn should value the loss of Katherine's household labor at its replacement cost. Since many of the household tasks did not require the use of Katherine's specialized skills, I use a more appropriate measure of replacement cost, the minimum wage.

- It is my opinion that, as a member of the Potter household, Katherine Potter consumed approximately 75 percent of her annual income as her personal consumption. The amount of consumption that Mrs. Potter consumed for her benefit out of her income should not be included in an award of damages to Mr. Potter as he did not necessarily benefit from this consumption during Mrs. Potter's lifetime. Although Mrs. Potter would continue to consume as a member of the household after her retirement, in order to be conservative in the estimate of damages, I exclude this amount from the calculation of loss to Mr. Potter. Inclusion of this stream of consumption of retirement would make the damages amount even smaller as Mrs. Potter would continue to consume but not be earning any wage or salary income.

In sum, these inappropriate and inaccurate assumptions used by Dr. Glenn in his model result in a significant overstatement of any likely damages suffered. I believe that he may have over-stated damages by as much as a factor of four. I believe that damages suffered by the plaintiff would not have exceeded $334,000.

5.0 Exhibits

For purposes of presenting our opinions and their bases, I may develop and use exhibits including overheads, flip charts, and other summary graphics. I may also use certain demonstrative aids and illustrations in presenting technical concepts and analyses.

6.0 Compensation

The hourly rates for myself and my research associates who worked on this matter range between $50 and $250 per hour. My hourly rate is $250 per hour.

Elizabeth C. Buchanan
Assistant Professor of Economics
Nita State University
Nita City, Nita
March 1, 2012

POTTER v. SHRACKLE AND THE SHRACKLE CONSTRUCTION COMPANY
REBUTTAL DAMAGES MODEL OF ELIZABETH C. BUCHANAN, PHD
TABLE 1. SUMMARY OF ECONOMIC LOSS, WRONGFUL DEATH OF
KATHERINE POTTER

Summary of Economic Loss

		Nominal Dollars	*Present Discounted Value*
A.	Future Value of Earnings	$807,964	$680,250
B.	Future Value of Fringe Benefits	$141,394	$119,044
c.	Future Value of Household Work	$68,500	$45,293
D.	Future Value of Personal Consumption	$606,781	$510,868
E.	Total Value of Loss (A+B+C-D)	$411,077	$333,719

POTTER v. SHRACKLE AND THE SHRACKLE CONSTRUCTION COMPANY
REBUTTAL DAMAGES MODEL OF ELIZABETH C. BUCHANAN, PHD
TABLE 2. FUTURE VALUE OF EARNINGS OF KATHERINE POTTER, AGE 45 TO 60

Date of Birth:	June 15, 1965
Date of Death:	December 4, 2010
Appraisal Period:	2011 to 2025
Projected Retirement Age:	55
Discount Rate:	6.00%
Earnings Growth Rate:	5.00%

Year	Projected Age	% of Full-Time Employment	Projected Value of Earnings	Present Discounted Value of Earnings
2010	45	100%	$85,000	
2011	46	100%	$89,252	$89,252
2012	47	100%	$93,717	$93,717
2013	48	100%	$98,405	$92,835
2014	49	100%	$103,328	$91,961
2015	50	100%	$108,497	$91,096
2016	51	50%	$56,962	$45,119
2017	52	50%	$59,811	$44,695
2018	53	50%	$62,803	$44,274
2019	54	50%	$65,945	$43,857
2020	55	50%	$69,244	$43,445
2021	56	0%	(RETIRED)	(RETIRED)
2022	57	0%	(RETIRED)	(RETIRED)
2023	58	0%	(RETIRED)	(RETIRED)
2024	59	0%	(RETIRED)	(RETIRED)
2025	60	0%	(RETIRED)	(RETIRED)
Value of Future Earnings:			$807,964	$680,250

POTTER v. SHRACKLE AND THE SHRACKLE CONSTRUCTION COMPANY
REBUTTAL DAMAGES MODEL OF ELIZABETH C. BUCHANAN, PHD
TABLE 3. HISTORICAL EARNINGS GROWTH OF KATHERINE POTTER,
1987 TO 2010

Date of Birth: June 15, 1965
Date of Death: December 4, 2010
Observation Period: 1987 TO 2010

Year	Age	Earnings	% Change from Previous Year	Job
1987to1989	22-24	$0	nla	(1)
1990	25	$19,000	nla	(2)
1991	26	$19,600	3.2%	(2)
1992	27	$20,250	3.3%	(2)
1993	28	$20,900	3.2%	(2)
1994	29	$21,600	3.3%	(2)
1995	30	$22,300	3.2%	(2)
1996	31	$23,000	3.1%	(2)
1997	32	$23,750	3.3%	(2)
1998	33	$24,500	3.2%	(2)
1999	34	$25,400	3.7%	(2)/(3)
2000	35	$34,000	33.9%	(3)
2001	36	$42,000	23.5%	(3)
2002	37	$50,000	19.0%	(3)
2003	38	$57,500	15.0%	(3)
2004	39	$62,500	8.7%	(3)
2005	40	$67,500	8.0%	(3)
2006	41	$71,000	5.2%	(3)
2007	42	$73,500	3.5%	(3)
2008	43	$76,000	3.4%	(3)
2009	44	$78,000	2.6%	(3)
2010	45	$85,000	9.0%	(3)
2011	Deceased	$0	-100.0%	Deceased

Average Income Growth Rate (2008 to 2010): 5.00%

Job Information:

(1)   Attending Graduate School, University of Nita
(2)   Computer Instructor, Nita City Unified School District
(3)   Computer Instructor, Techno-Soft, Inc.

POTTER v. SHRACKLE AND THE SHRACKLE CONSTRUCTION COMPANY REBUTTAL DAMAGES MODEL OF ELIZABETH C. BUCHANAN, PHD
TABLE 4. FUTURE VALUE OF FRINGE BENEFITS OF KATHERINE POTTER, AGE 45 TO 60

Date of Birth:	June 15, 1965
Date of Death:	December 4, 2010
Appraisal Period:	2011 to 2025
Projected Retirement Age:	55
Discount Rate:	6.00%
Benefits as % of Income:	17.50%

Year	ProjectedAge	Projected Value of Fringe Benefits	Present Discounted Value of Fringe Benefits
2010	45	$14,875	
2011	46	$15,619	$15,619
2012	47	$16,400	$16,400
2013	48	$17,221	$16,246
2014	49	$18,082	$16,093
2015	50	$18,987	$15,942
2016	51	$9,968	$7,896
2017	52	$10,467	$7,822
2018	53	$10,991	$7,748
2019	54	$11,540	$7,675
2020	55	$12,118	$7,603
2021	56	(RETIRED)	(RETIRED)
2022	51	(RETIRED)	(RETIRED)
2023	58	(RETIRED)	(RETIRED)
2024	59	(RETIRED)	(RETIRED)
2025	60	(RETIRED)	(RETIRED)
Value of Future Fringe Benefits:		$141,394	$119,044

POTTER v. SHRACKLE AND THE SHRACKLE CONSTRUCTION COMPANY
REBUTTAL DAMAGES MODEL OF ELIZABETH C. BUCHANAN, PHD
TABLE 5. FUTURE VALUE OF HOUSEHOLD WORK OF KATHERINE POTTER,
AGE 45 TO 60

Date of Birth:	June 15, 1965
Date of Death:	December 4, 2010
Appraisal Period:	2011 to 2025
Projected Retirement Age:	55
Discount Rate:	6.00%

	Before Retirement	Retirement
# of Hours Per Day at Household Work:	2	4
Days Per Year Doing Household Work:	250	250
Total Hours Per Year	500	1000

Year	Projected Age	Hourly Replacement Wage for Household Work	Projected Value of Household Work	Present Discounted Value of Household Work	
2010	45	$6.00	$3,000		
2011	46	$6.00	$3,000	$3,000	
2012	47	$6.00	$3,000	$3,000	
2013	48	$6.00	$3,000	$2,830	
2014	49	$6.00	$3,000	$2,670	
2015	50	$6.50	$3,250	$2,729	
2016	51	$6.50	$3,250	$2,574	
2017	52	$6.50	$3,250	$2,429	
2018	53	$6.50	$3,250	$2,291	
2019	54	$7.00	$3,500	$2,328	
2020	55	$7.00	$3,500	$2,196	
2021	56	$7.00	$7,000	$4,143	(RETIRED)
2022	57	$7.00	$7,000	$3,909	(RETIRED)
2023	58	$7.50	$7,500	$3,951	(RETIRED)
2024	59	$7.50	$7,500	$3,727	(RETIRED)
2025	60	$7.50	$7,500	$3,516	(RETIRED)
Value of Future Household Work:			$68,500	$45,293	

POTTER v. SHRACKLE AND THE SHRACKLE CONSTRUCTION COMPANY
REBUTTAL DAMAGES MODEL OF ELIZABETH C. BUCHANAN, PHD
TABLE 6. FUTURE VALUE OF PERSONAL CONSUMPTION OF KATHERINE POTTER, AGE 45 TO 60

Date of Birth:	June 15, 1965
Date of Death:	December 4, 2010
Appraisal Period:	2011 to 2025
Projected Retirement Age:	55
Discount Rate:	6.00%
Consumption as % of Full-Time Income:	75.10%

Year	Projected Age	Projected Value of Personal Consumption	Present Discounted Value of Personal Consumption
2010	45	$63,835	
2011	46	$67,028	67,028
2012	47	$70,381	70,381
2013	48	$73,902	69,719
2014	49	$77,599	69,063
2015	50	$81,481	68,413
2016	51	$42,778	33,885
2017	52	$44,918	33,566
2018	53	$47,165	33,250
2019	54	$49,525	32,937
2020	55	$52,002	32,627
2021	56	(Retired)	(Retired)
2022	57	(Retired)	(Retired)
2023	58	(Retired)	(Retired)
2024	59	(Retired)	(Retired)
2025	60	(Retired)	(Retired)
Value of Future Consumption:		$606,781	$510,868

Dr. Elizabeth C. Buchanan

Business Address: Department of Economics, DB #234
Nita State University, CB# 233
Nita City, Nita
(555) 555-4387
Fax: (555) 555-4388
E-mail: ebuchan@email.nsu.edu

Education: BS, University of Nita, 1997 (economics)
PhD University of Nita, 2001 (economics)

Current position: Assistant Professor of Economics, Nita State University. Concentration in labor economics and industrial organization.

Employment history: Assistant Professor of Economics, Nita State University since 2006.

Dunhill Consultants, private economics consulting group, 2001-2006.

Principal publications since 2001:

"The Value of Household Services," 18 Journal of Labor Economics 284 (2003)

"Damage Assessment for the Infringement of Intellectual Property Rights," 82 Contemporary

Economics Problems 1204 (2007)

"Economic Loss in Copyright Cases," 4 Journal of Law and Economics 48 (2008)

"Can We Accurately Evaluate Lost Wages?" 7 Journal of Law and Economics 87 (2010)

"Intellectual Property and Modern Economic Thought," 80 Harvard Public Policy Review 438 (2011)

Expert Testimony: Homer v. Underhill, Nita Superior Court, June 2006 (personal injury case, testified for the plaintiff with regard to economic loss resulting from injury)

Glandon v. Schwartz, Nita Superior Court, May, 2008 (wrongful death case, testified for defendant with regard to economic loss resulting from death)

Marydale v. Farrer, Nita Superior Court, September, 2010 (personal injury case, testified for the defendant with regard to economic loss resulting from injury)

MEMORANDUM

To: Robert Glenn, PhD

From: Steve Dyer, Research Assistant

Date: September 16, 2011

Re: Potter v. Shrackle

CONFIDENTIAL

Per your request, I've read through Dr. Buchanan's expert report in the Potter case. Contrasting her analysis with yours, I think the following points are important.

First, Dr. Buchanan assumes that Katherine Potter will completely stop working at age 55. In his deposition, Daniel Sloan, her boss, stated that "She told me that there was no way that she would retire before she was sixty." Dr. Buchanan doesn't address this testimony in her expert report. In fact, the deposition testimony of Jeffrey Potter indicates that, although he mentioned early retirement to her, Katherine did not agree to it.

Second, Dr. Buchanan does not include the possibility that Mrs. Potter might have been promoted, which would have resulted in an increase in Mrs. Potter's annual salary. Mr. Sloan mentioned in his deposition that his "business is expanding" and "Mrs. Potter was exactly the kind of person" the business needed because "she had all of the technical skills as well as an extraordinary ability to work with people." Mr. Sloan even goes as far as saying that he "was grooming her to become an executive vice-president." This indicates that it is very likely that Mrs. Potter would have been promoted before she retired and would have received a commensurate boost in her salary. Dr. Buchanan assumes that she wouldn't be promoted and her salary growth would be stagnant.

Third, Dr. Buchanan understates the value of Mrs. Potter's fringe benefits as a percentage of her annual salary. She uses 17.5 percent of Mrs. Potter's salary to calculate benefits. However, the actual amount of benefits, excluding the $2,000 bonus, is closer to 17.65 percent. Even though it is probably not a large difference in terms of damages, it is an inaccuracy in her report. More importantly, I believe your estimates using 20 percent for the fringe benefits package is correct. In his deposition, Daniel Sloan states, "At the time of her death, her fringe benefits package was 20 percent of her salary. This included contribution to a retirement plan, medical and dental insurance, as well as life and disability insurance." Based upon this statement, the $2,000 bonus is not included in the 20 percent which Mr. Sloan talks about. I think Dr. Buchanan was confused when she talked to Linda Graham and thought the $2,000 was included in Mr. Sloan's 20 percent figure for fringe benefits.

Fourth, Dr. Buchanan uses minimum wage as the replacement cost for the loss of Mrs. Potter's household labor. Some household chores, however, should be valued at more than the minimum wage, such as cooking and gardening, as Mr. Potter really could not find somebody to do such things for minimum wage. In addition, to the extent that Mrs. Potter had specialized skills (such as managing the household finances, preparing tax returns, etc.), the value of her lost work should be valued at its replacement cost, which would likely be higher than minimum wage.

On the other hand, I note in your report that you use Mrs. Potter's imputed hourly wage at Techno-Soft, Inc. to value her lost household work. I think the calculation comes out to be somewhere around $41 per hour for her imputed wage. Even if Dr. Buchanan underestimates the value of Mrs. Potter's lost household work using the hourly minimum wage, I think using her imputed Techno-Soft, Inc. wage may overstate the value of her lost household work insofar as it would not take someone making $41 per hour to do basic, unskilled household work.

Fifth, both you and Dr. Buchanan use the same discount rate in your calculations.

Sixth, both you and Dr. Buchanan use the same consumption rate in your calculations.

I will continue to look for more documents that can better support our arguments. In the meantime, I will come by your office later in the week so that you can approve my time sheet.

Jury Instructions

Preliminary Instructions

1. Introduction

You have been selected as jurors and have taken an oath to well and truly try this case. This trial will last one day.

During the progress of the trial there will be periods of time when the Court recesses. During those periods of time, you must not talk about this case among yourselves or with anyone else. Do not talk to any of the parties, their lawyers, or any of the witnesses.

You should keep an open mind. You should not form or express an opinion during the trial and should reach no conclusion in this case until you have heard all of the evidence, the arguments of counsel, and the final instructions as to the law that will be given to you by the Court.

2. Conduct of the Trial

First, the attorneys will have an opportunity to make opening statements. These statements are not evidence and should be considered only as a preview of what the attorneys expect the evidence will be.

Following the opening statements, witnesses will be called to testify. They will be placed under oath and questioned by the attorneys. Documents and other tangible exhibits may also be received as evidence. If an exhibit is given to you to examine, you should examine it carefully, individually, and without any comment.

It is counsel's right and duty to object when testimony or other evidence is being offered that he or she believes is not admissible.

When the Court sustains an objection to a question, the jurors must disregard the question and the answer, if one has been given, and draw no inference from the question or answer or speculate as to what the witness would have said if permitted to answer. Jurors must also disregard evidence stricken from the record.

When the Court sustains an objection to any evidence the jurors must disregard that evidence. When the Court overrules an objection to any evidence, the jurors must not give that evidence any more weight than if the objection had not been made.

When the evidence is completed, the attorneys will make final statements. These final statements are not evidence but are given to assist you in evaluating the evidence. The attorneys are also permitted to argue in an attempt to persuade you to a particular verdict. You may accept or reject those arguments as you see fit.

Finally, just before you retire to consider your verdict, I will give you further instructions on the law that applies to this case

Final Instructions

1.   Members of the jury, the evidence and arguments in this case have been completed, and I will now instruct you as to the law.

The laws applicable to this case are stated in these instructions and it is your duty to follow all of them. You must not single out certain instructions and disregard others.

It is your duty to determine the facts, and to determine them only from the evidence in this case. You are to apply the law to the facts and in this way decide the case. You must not be governed or influenced by sympathy or prejudice for or against any party in this case. Your verdict must be based on evidence and not upon speculation, guess, or conjecture.

From time to time the court has ruled on the admissibility of evidence. You must not concern yourselves with the reasons for these rulings. You should disregard questions and exhibits that were withdrawn or to which objections were sustained.

You should also disregard testimony and exhibits that the court has refused or stricken. The evidence that you should consider consists only of the witnesses' testimonies and the exhibits the court has received.

Any evidence that was received for a limited purpose should not be considered by you for any other purpose.

You should consider all the evidence in the light of your own observations and experiences in life.

Neither by these instructions nor by any ruling or remark that I have made do I mean to indicate any opinion as to the facts or as to what your verdict should be.

2.   You are the sole judges of the credibility of the witnesses and of the weight to be given to the testimony of each witness. In determining what credit is to be given any witness, you may take into account his or her ability and opportunity to observe; his or her manner and appearance while testifying; any interest, bias, or prejudice he or she may have; the reasonableness of the testimony considered in the light of all the evidence; and any other factors that bear on the believability and weight of the witness' testimony.

3.   You have heard evidence in this case from witnesses who testified as experts. The law allows experts to express an opinion on subjects involving their special knowledge, training and skill, experience, or research. While their opinions are allowed to be given, it is entirely within the province of the jury to determine what weight shall be given their testimony. Jurors are not bound by the testimony of experts; their testimony is to be weighed as that of any other witness.

4.   The law recognizes two kinds of evidence: direct and circumstantial. Direct evidence proves a fact directly; that is, the evidence by itself, if true, establishes the fact. Circumstantial evidence is the proof of facts or circumstances that give rise to a reasonable inference of other facts; that is, circumstantial evidence proves a fact indirectly in that it follows from other facts or circumstances according to common experience and observations in life. An eyewitness is a common example of direct evidence, while human footprints are circumstantial evidence that a person was present.

The law makes no distinction between direct and circumstantial evidence as to the degree or amount of proof required, and each should be considered according to whatever weight or value it may have. All of the evidence should be considered and evaluated by you in arriving at your verdict.

5.   When I say that a party has the burden of proof on any issue, or use the expression "if you find," "if you decide," or "by a preponderance of the evidence," I mean that you must be persuaded from a consideration of all the evidence in the case that the issue in question is more probably true than not true.

Any findings of fact you make must be based on probabilities, not possibilities. They may not be based on surmise, speculation, or conjecture.

6.   One of the parties in this case is a corporation, and it is entitled to the same fair treatment as an individual would be entitled to under like circumstances, and you should decide the case with the same impartiality you would use in deciding a case between individuals.

7.   The Court will now instruct you on the claims and defenses of each party and the law governing the case. You must arrive at your verdict by unanimous vote, applying the law, as you are now instructed, to the facts as you find them to be.

8.   Plaintiff claims that Charles Shrackle was negligent in his operation and control of the pickup truck and that his negligence caused Katherine Potter's injuries and death. Plaintiff seeks damages for defendants' negligence both on behalf of himself individually and as the administrator of Katherine Potter's estate. Thus, plaintiff has brought this lawsuit and is claiming damages in two separate capacities: (1) as an individual for the injury and loss suffered by him as Katherine Potter's husband, and (2) as the administrator of Katherine Potter's estate for the pain, suffering, and expenses incurred by her prior to her death.

Defendants deny that Charles Shrackle was negligent or that his negligence caused Katherine Potter's injuries and death. Defendants claim that Katherine Potter was negligent, and that it was her own negligence that caused her injuries and death.

9.   In this case, the plaintiff, Jeffrey Potter, has the burden of proving:

(1)   That Charles Shrackle was negligent, and;

(2)   That the negligence of Charles Shrackle proximately caused Katherine Potter's death.

The defendants have the burden of proving:

(1)   That the deceased, Katherine Potter, was negligent, and;

(2)   That the negligence of Katherine Potter was a proximate cause of her death.

Thus, each of the parties to this case has a burden of proof to maintain, and you are to determine whether they have met their burdens. Your task is to determine whether Charles Shrackle or Katherine Potter, or both, were negligent, and the extent to which their negligence caused Katherine Potter's injuries and death.

10.   The terms "negligent" or "negligence" as used in these instructions mean the failure to use that degree of care that an ordinarily careful and prudent person would use under the same or similar circumstances.

11. The terms "contributorily negligent" or "contributory negligence" mean negligence on the part of the deceased Katherine Potter.

12. It is the duty of every person using a public street or highway, whether a pedestrian or a driver of a vehicle, to exercise ordinary care to avoid placing himself, herself, or others in danger and to exercise ordinary care to avoid a collision.

13. The violation of a statute, if you find any, is negligence as a matter of law. Such negligence has the same effect as any other act or acts of negligence.

A statute in the state of Nita provides:

(1) That the driver of a motor vehicle shall yield the right of way, by slowing down or stopping if necessary, to a pedestrian crossing the roadway within a crosswalk when the pedestrian is upon that half of the roadway in which the vehicle is traveling, or when either the vehicle or the pedestrian is approaching that half of the roadway so closely that the pedestrian is in danger.

(2) That a pedestrian crossing a roadway at any point other than within a marked crosswalk shall yield the right of way to all vehicles upon the roadway.

(3) This right of way, however, is not absolute but rather creates a duty to exercise ordinary care to avoid collisions upon the party having the right of way.

14. Proximate cause is that cause which, in a natural and continuous sequence, produces the injury, and without which the injury would not have occurred.

To be a proximate cause of Katherine Potter's injuries and death, negligent conduct by either Charles Shrackle or Katherine Potter need not be the only cause, nor the last or nearest cause. It is sufficient if the negligent conduct acting concurrently with another cause produced the injury.

Thus, there need not be only one proximate cause of Katherine Potter's injuries and death, and you may find that the negligence of both Charles Shrackle and Katherine Potter was the proximate cause of her death. On the other hand, you may find that the negligence of either of them was the sole proximate cause of her death.

15. You are to determine the negligence, if any, of both Charles Shrackle and Katherine Potter, and then to apportion the responsibility of each.

Please state your findings of negligence in the following form:

We find the conduct of the defendant, Charles Shrackle, was _____ % negligent.

We find that the conduct of the deceased, Katherine Potter, was _____ % negligent.

16. In this case you must also decide the issue of damages. You must determine the amount which will reasonably and fairly compensate Jeffrey Potter for the losses resulting from the death of his wife, Katherine Potter.

In determining the loss to the plaintiff, Jeffrey Potter, you should consider the following factors:

(1) Expenses for care, treatment, and hospitalization incident to the injury to Katherine Potter resulting in her death;

(2) Compensation for the pain and suffering of the decedent;

(3) The reasonable funeral expenses of the decedent;

(4) The present monetary value of the decedent to the persons entitled to receive the damages recovered, including but not limited to compensation for the loss of the reasonably expected:

    (a) net income of the decedent;

    (b)· services, protection, care, and assistance of the decedent, whether voluntary or obligatory, to the persons entitled to the damages recovered;

    (c) society, companionship, comfort, guidance, kindly offices, and advice of the decedent to the persons entitled to the damages recovered;

(5) Nominal damages when the jury so finds.

17. In determining the amount of damages to the plaintiff, you may consider how long the plaintiff is likely to live, how long the decedent was likely to have lived, that some persons work all their lives and others do not, that a person's earnings may remain the same or may increase or decrease in the future.

In calculating the amount of damages, you must not simply multiply the life expectancies by the annual damages. Instead, you must determine the present cash value for any award of damages. "Present cash value" means the sum of money needed now, which together with what that sum will earn in the future, will equal the amount of the benefits at the times in the future when they would have been received.

18. The Court did not in any way, and does not by these instructions, give or intimate any opinions as to what has or has not been proven in the case, or as to what are or are not the facts of the case.

No one of these instructions states all of the law applicable, but all of them must be taken, read, and considered together as they are connected with and related to each other as a whole.

You must not be concerned with the wisdom of any rule of law. Regardless of any opinions you may have as to what the law ought to be, it would be a violation of your sworn duty to base a verdict upon any other view of the law than that given in the instructions of the court.

IN THE CIRCUIT COURT OF
DARROW COUNTY, NITA
CIVIL DIVISION

Jeffrey T. Potter, the	)	
Administrator of the Estate, and	)	
of Katherine Potter,	)	
Jeffrey T. Potter, individually,	)	
	)	Jury Verdict
Plaintiffs,	)	(Interrogatories)
	)	
v.	)	
	)	
Charles T. Shrackle and	)	
The Shrackle Construction Company,	)	
	)	
Defendants.	)	

The jury is to answer the following interrogatories. The foreperson is to answer the interrogatories for the jury and sign the verdict.

Interrogatory No. 1:

Please state your findings of negligence in the following form:

We find that the conduct of the defendant, Charles T. Shrackle, was _____% negligent.

We find that the conduct of the deceased, Katherine Potter, was _____% negligent.

Interrogatory No. 2:

Please determine the amount of damages to the plaintiff, Jeffrey T. Potter, both individually and as administrator of Katherine Potter's estate:

Amount _____$

The percentage of negligence that you find to be apportioned to the defendant, Charles T. Shrackle (Interrogatory No.1) is multiplied by the amount of damages you determine (Interrogatory No. 2), and that amount will be the verdict for the plaintiff, Jeffrey T. Potter.

The members of the jury have unanimously answered the interrogatories in the manner that I have indicated.

_____
Foreperson

Exhibit 1

Department of Transportation
Bureau of Safety
Programing and Analysis
T&S Building, Nita City, Nita

NITA POLICE DEPARTMENT TRAFFIC ACCIDENT REPORT

Page 1 of 2

Investigating Officer/ Badge No.	Michael Young / #7319		Date of Report	12/6/10		Approved By/ Date	
Date	11/30/10	Time	3:28	County	Darrow	City	Nita City
No. Vehicles	1	No. Killed	1	No. Injuried		Municipality	

Principal Road   Intersecting Road

Street Name	Mattis	Speed Limit		Street Name		Speed Limit	

Nearest Cross Street Kirby   Check if One Way ☐ N ☐ S ☐ E ☐ W   Direction From Accident Site ☐ N ☐ S ☐ E ☐ W

Illumination	Weather	Road Surface	Traffic Control Device Type	
☐ Dawn or Dusk	☒ No Adverse Conditions	☒ Dry	☐ No Controls	☐ RR Crossing Controls
☒ Daylight	☐ Raining	☐ Wet	☐ Flashing Traffic Signal	☐ Police Officer/Flagman
☐ Dark (with street lights)	☐ Sleet/Hail	☐ Muddy	☒ Traffic Signal	☐ Flashing School Zone Sign
☐ Dark (with no street lights)	☐ Snowing	☐ Snow/Ice	☐ Stop Sign	☐ Other
	☐ Fog/Smoke		☐ Yield Sign	

Vehicle Driver No. 1

☒ Moving   ☐ Stopped in Traffic   ☐ Parked   ☐ Pedestrian   ☐ Bicyclist   ☐ Other

Drivers Name (First, Middle, Last)	Charles T. Shrackle		Divers License Number		State	
Street Address	1701 W Johnston			Date of Birth	5/13/73	
City	Nita City	State Nita	Zip Code	Telephone Numbers		
Vehicle (Year/Make)	2001 Toyota pickup	License Plate or ID Number		State	Nita	
Vehicle Owner	Charles T. Shrackle			Date of Birth		
Address		City		State		Zip Code

Vehicle Driver No. 2

☐ Moving   ☐ Stopped in Traffic   ☐ Parked   ☒ Pedestrian   ☐ Bicyclist   ☐ Other

Drivers Name (First, Middle, Last)	Katherine Potter		Divers License Number		State	
Street Address	4920 Thorndale Avenue			Date of Birth		
City	Nita City	State Nita	Zip Code	Telephone Numbers		
Vehicle (Year/Make)		License Plate or ID Number		State		
Vehicle Owner				Date of Birth		
Address		City		State		Zip Code

Department of Transportation
Bureau of Safety
Programing and Analysis
T&S Building, Nita City, Nita

NITA POLICE DEPARTMENT TRAFFIC ACCIDENT REPORT

Witnesses

(A) Juanita and Vicky Williams
    1010 W Kirby #15
    Nita

(B) Marilyn Kelly
    1910 Elden Lane
    Nita

Narrative

#1 was southbound on Mattis after turning left from Kirby. He then struck #2 (pedestrian) approx 30 feet S of pedestrian crosswalk. #1 said he didn't see pedestrian until after he struck her. Witnesses A (mother & daughter) had been in car driving east on Kirby and saw pedestrian running across street westbound. Neither saw actual contact.

On 12/2/10 witness B called station and said pedestrian was in crosswalk.

On 12/5/10 I was informed that pedestrian had died.

Diagram

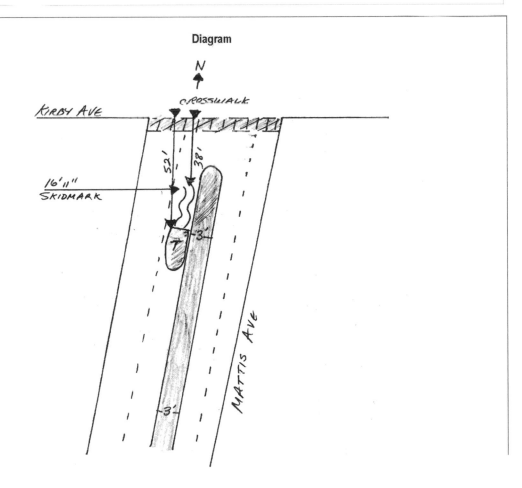

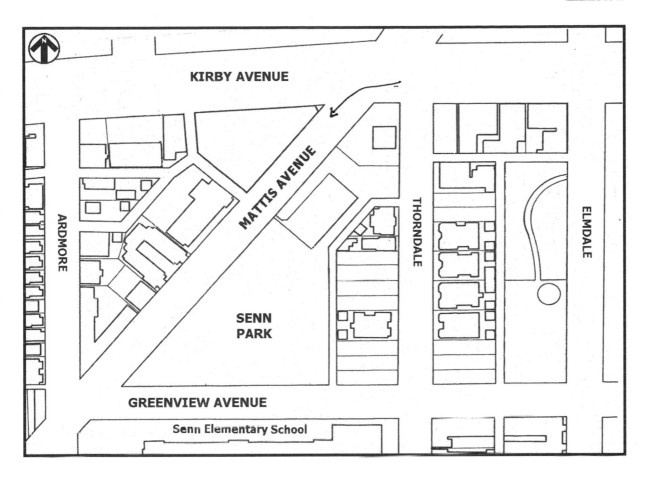

Exhibit 2a

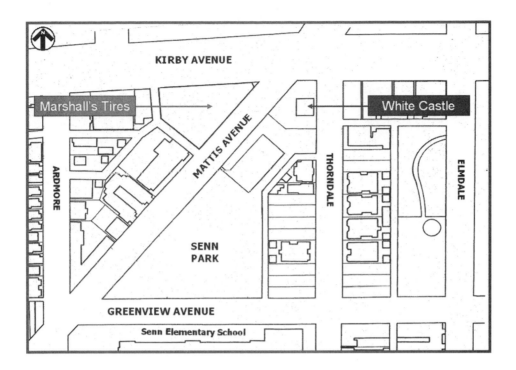

Exhibit 2b

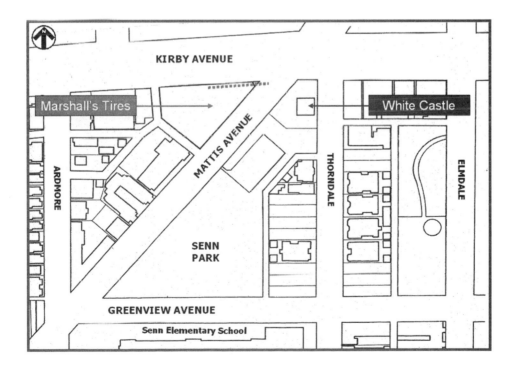

Exhibit 2c

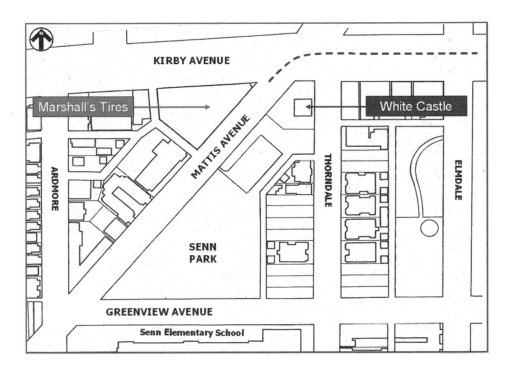

Exhibit 2d

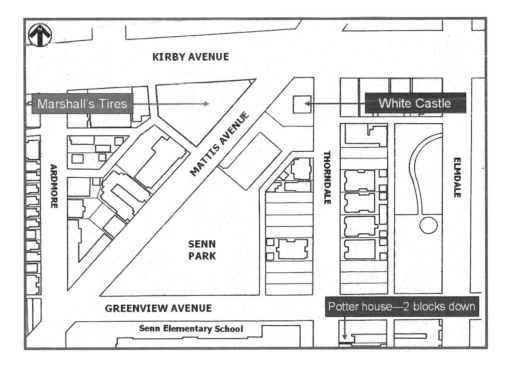

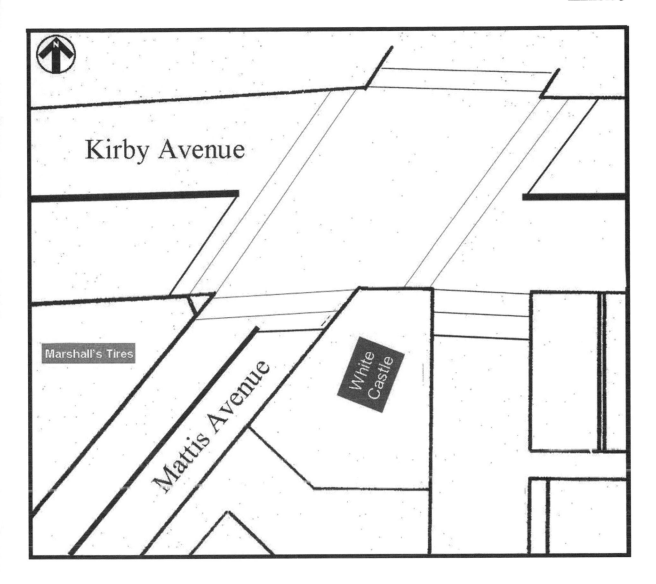

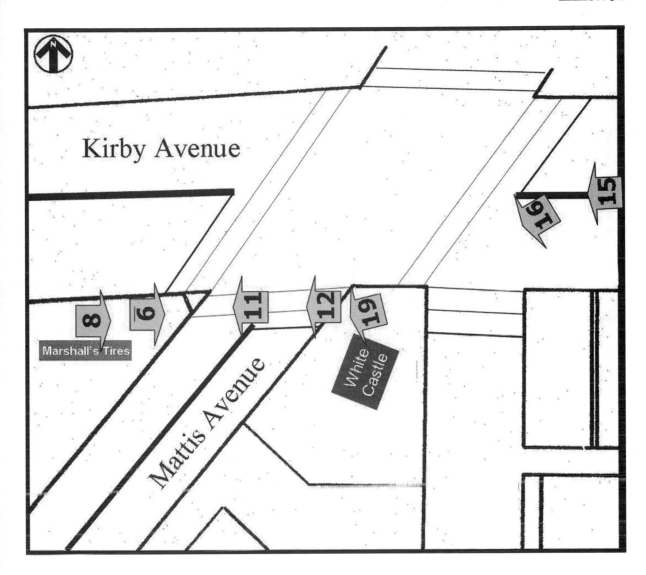

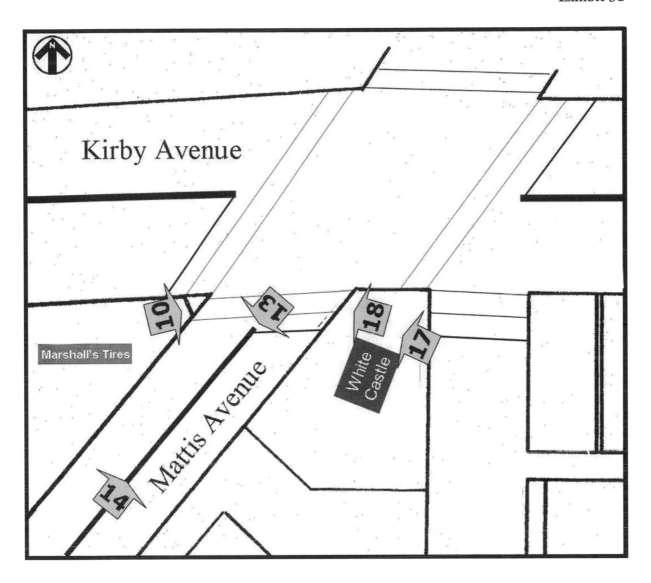

Exhibit 3a

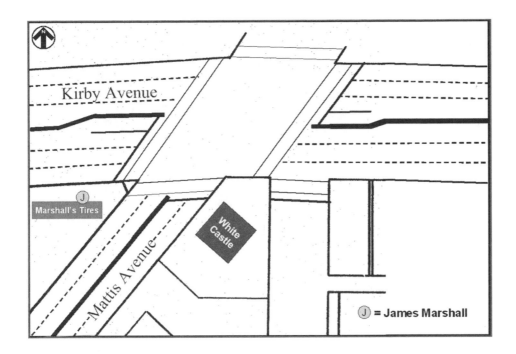

Exhibit 3b

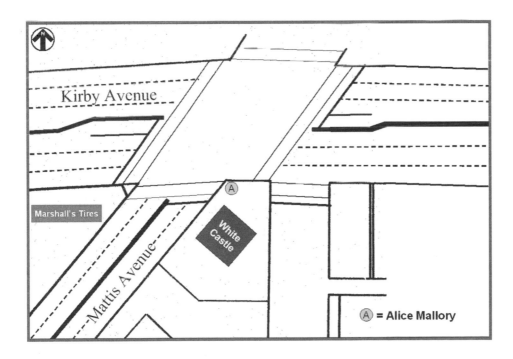

Exhibit 3c

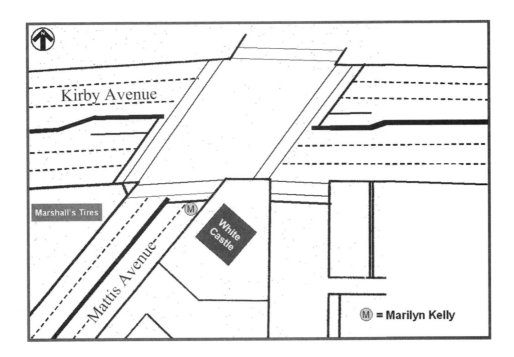

Exhibit 3d

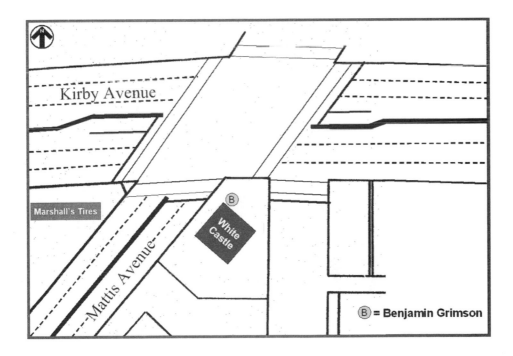

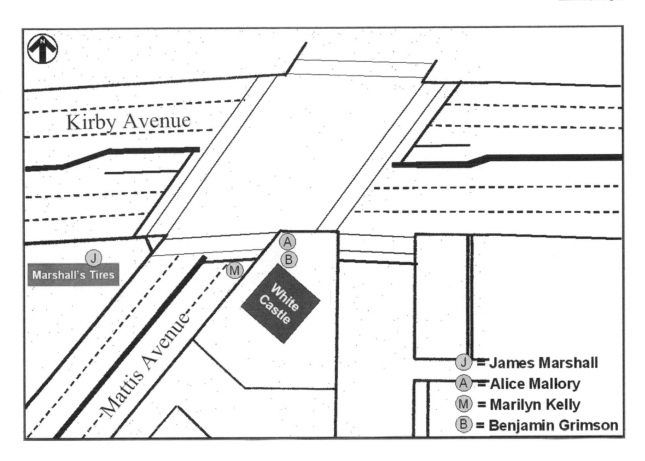

Exhibit 5

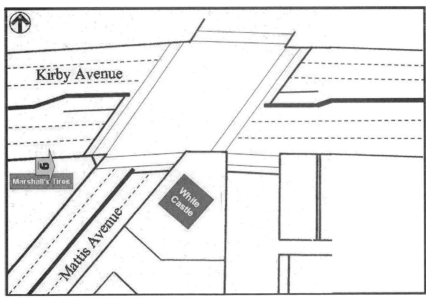

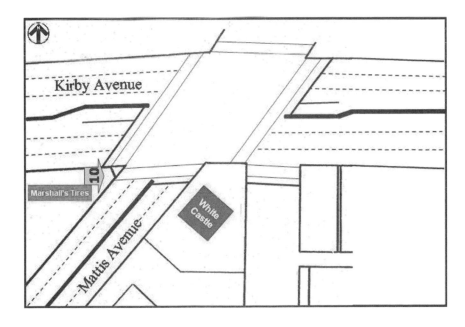

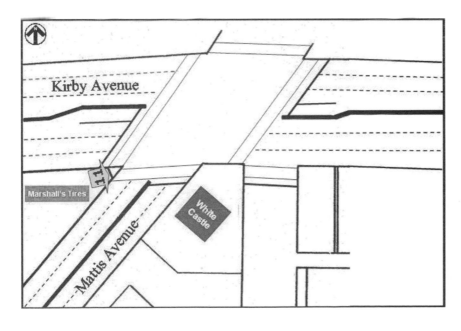

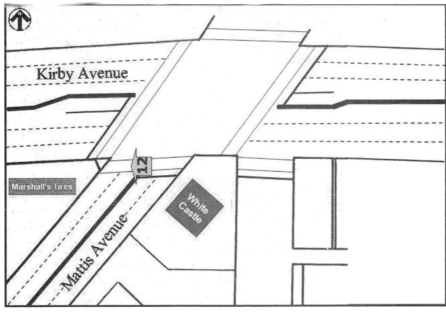

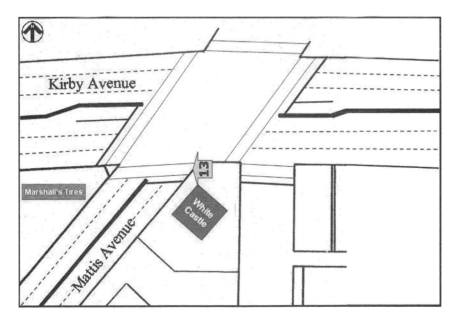

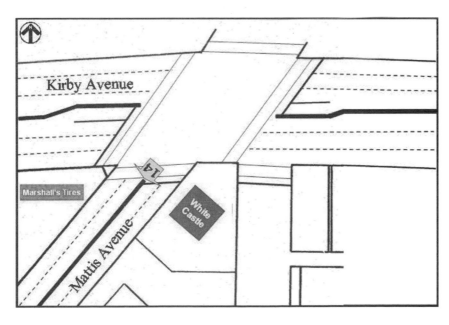

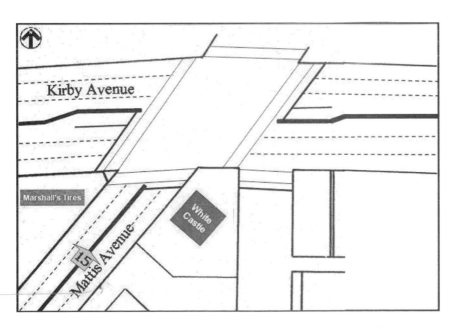

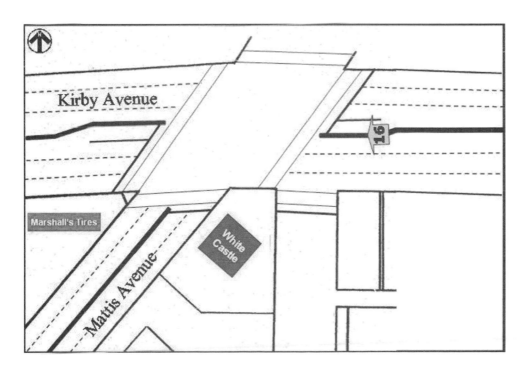

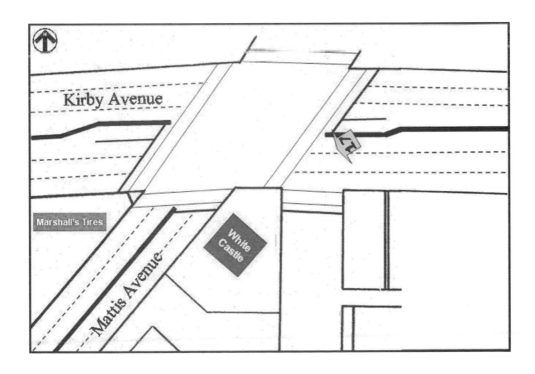

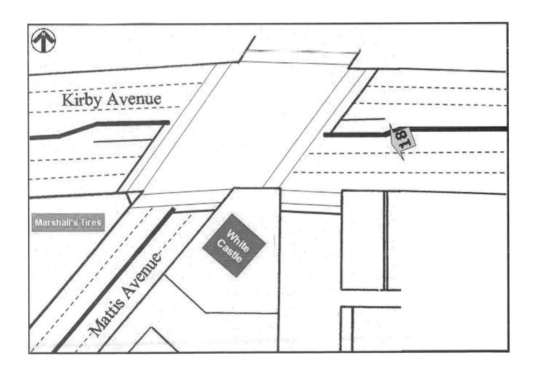

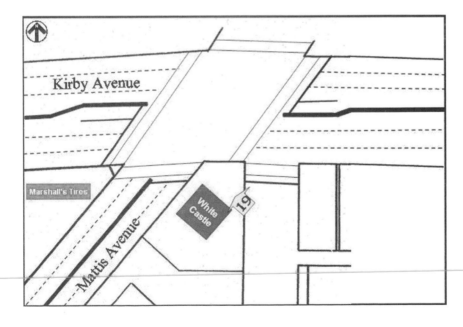

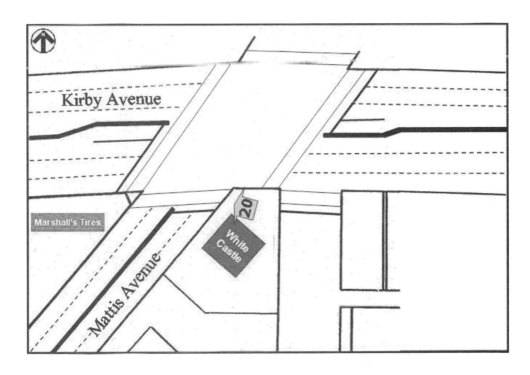

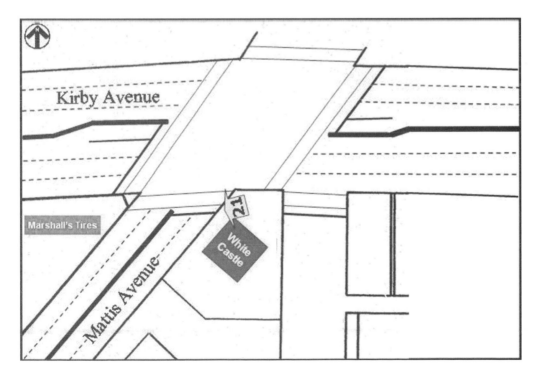

Statement of James Marshall

I am the owner-operator of Jim Marshall's
JM tires, ~~1601~~ (~~1610~~) Kirby, Nita City, Nita. I was
working in the car wash portion of my
business on Nov. 30, 2010.

At approximately 3:30 on Nov. 30, 2010,
I was doing some maintenance work on
one of the vacuum units for the car wash.
JM It was the ~~first~~ (second) from the corner. I saw
a dark-haired woman walking east on the
south sidewalk of Kirby. When I saw her,
she was 15 or 20 feet from the intersection.
I looked over at my employee, Ed Putnam,
to ask him something about the job we
were doing. About a minute or minute
and a half later I heard a thump.
I looked out and saw a pickup truck
carrying a body on the front of it.
I sent Putnam out to see if he could
be of help while I called the police.
I went out to see if I could be of
help and saw the same woman that
I'd seen earlier walking east on
Kirby lying on the pavement.

Signed: James Marshall
Witness: Joseph Lucey
Dec. 12, 2010

Marshall's business is located on the southwest corner of Kirby and Mattis. This statement was taken by Joseph Lucey, an adjuster for the defendant's insurance carrier, on December 12, 2010, at about 11 a.m. The statement was written by Mr. Lucey. The signature and the correction are in Marshall's handwriting.

Exhibit 23

Clark Poe

_____

From: Clark Poe <cpoe@poecon.nita>
Sent: Monday, November 29, 2010 9:34 AM
To: Charles Shrackle
Subject: Greenbriar

Charlie: The delays on the Greenbriar project are unacceptable. We are so far behind that the developer, Mr. Green, is about ready to cancel the job and get a new contractor. Legally, he can probably do it.

I know that you've had some trouble with rock, but there is always trouble with rock in this area. We need to finish this job immediately!

Come to the job site at 3:30 p.m. on November 30 and be ready to give me a detailed description of your problems and a firm commitment on a conclusion date. This has become a real problem, Charlie, so be there and be on time.

Clark
Clark Poe Construction Company
414 Whitebread Road
Nita City, Nita 99992
(555) 828-1891
cpoe@poecon.nita

Exhibit 24

Charles T. Shrackle

From: Charles T. Shrackle <cts@shrackleconstruction.nita>
Sent: Monday, November 29, 2010 10:23 AM
To: Clark Poe (cpoe@poecon.nita)
Subject: Greenbriar

Clark: I hear you loud and clear. I'll be there at 3:30 tomorrow. Unlike sometimes in the past, I assure you I won't be late.

Charlie

Charles T. Shrackle
Shrackle Construction Company
Route 45
Sommers Township
Nita City, Nita 99994
(555) 826-9406

Exhibit 25

Nita City Weather Channel
www.ncweather.nita

Weather report for Nita City, Nita on November 30, 2010

Sunny
56°
Chance of Rain: 0%
Wind: W at 11 mph
Sunny skies. High 56F. Winds W at 10 to 15 mph.

Sunrise: 6:55 am	**Sunset:** 4:21 pm

Exhibit 26

NMH Nita Memorial Hospital

444 Medway Park Circle Nita City, Nita 40088 (555)555-4444

SF-1Statement

Please note: This is a short form statement listing general charges. Itemization statements are available upon request for all services and goods provided.

Statement date:	12/7/10	
Patient:	Katherine Potter (deceased)	
Patient ID:	4478-622-00	
Admitted:	Yes	
Time/date of initial treatment:	4:18 p.m., 11/30/10	
ER attending physician:	Ashley P. Smith, MD #609:	
Other physician(s):	Kevin M. Patterson, MD #711	
Brief description:	Severe head trauma, brain injury, and fractured skull; result of being struck by moving vehicle. Intermittent consciousness; surgery to relieve pressure on brain	
Release date:	TOD 12/4/2010, 4 p.m.	

11/30/10	NMH ambulance run service	$840
11/30/10	Emergency room	$4,500
	ER physician (Ref: Ashley P. Smith, MD #609)	$4,080
	Medications administered	$1,660
11/30/10-12/4/2010	Intensive care private room and attendant care 5 days @ $17,000	$84,200
	Physician, surgery 12/1/10 medications; tests; blood, IV	$11,720
12/4/2010	NMH morgue service	$800
	Total:	$107,800

This statement is for general billing information only and not intended for insurance submission. Insurance claims may be pending and are not necessarily reflected on this statement. Itemizations of all charges are available upon request.

Odell Funeral Home

2002 Eternity Way, Nita City, Nita

(555) 555-7734

Confidential Invoice

INVOICE DATE: January 12, 2010

SERVICES FOR: Katherine Potter, December 11, 2010

20-gauge reinforced steel "Norabella" casket, sealed	$	8,000
heavy duty gasket, screw lock, seal kit		229
delivery included		
General prep services		600
additional prep		200
Silk flower casket spray (blue, white, gold)		200
Memorial stone		2,300
photo etched		375
"Restful Garden" Mausoleum, unit 40		3,000
Peace Garden Cemetery, Nita City, service fee		980
Limousine 2 hours @ 270.50/hour		541
10-inch obituary in Nita Journal-Gazette with photo		75
TOTAL DUE, NET 30:	$	16,500.00

Established 1924

Exhibit 28

4920 Thorndale Avenue
Nita City, Nita 99993
September 2, 2010

Dr. Andrew Stevens
Stevens Counseling
1225 North Street
Lisle, Nita 99980

Dear Dr. Stevens:

I am sorry that payment for our last three sessions is late. I guess it goes without saying that Katherine and I don't see eye to eye on the need for this counseling, and it is very difficult for me to get her to even speak calmly about it, much less agree for us to pay for it.

Nonetheless, I am enclosing our check in the amount of $300.

I am sorry that we can't continue with you. I thought your advice was very helpful and I appreciated the opportunity to talk with you about the problems that we have been having. I especially want to thank you for your concern about the early retirement issue. Eventhough Katherine loves her career, I am confident she would like the leisurely life of a college professor's wife even more. When we first got married, I was unable to talk her into having children. She was too career-driven. I hope that I can make more headway on the retirement issue.

Your comments at the last session that it was obvious to you that Katherine and I loved each other very much and would come out of this stronger than ever, make me smile and look forward to the future. I am sure that you are right. Perhaps when we have more time and her career isn't so hectic, I'll be able to persuade Katherine to come back with me to talk to you about the rest of our problems, which don't seem quite so important now. Despite all of the difficulties, I believe that our marriage will work. If it doesn't, so be it. If we can't resolve things, I can leave the marriage and seek a relationship that fulfills my needs.

In any event, keep your fingers crossed for us, please. Sincerely yours,

Jeffrey T. Potter

Jeffrey T. Potter

Exhibit 29

NITA TRAVEL COMPANY   eTICKET RECEIPT

Reservation Code:	WQMFKA	Issuing Agent:	Nita City, Nita
Ticket Number:	8675309502425	Issuing Agent:	3BA78/4076
Issuing Airline:	CARIBBEAN AIRLINES	IATA number:	66397478
Date Issued:	30May11	Invoice number:	483228
Customer Number:	8972509574		
Passenger:	Jeffrey Potter		

14JUN11 Caribbean Air CA 1066	Seat 15B	
From: Nita City, Nita (Nita City Intern'l)	Departs: 730A	Business Confirmed
To: Fort de France, Martinique (FDF)	Arrives: 355P	Fare Basis: TC8BX
		Not Valid Before: 14JUN
		Not Valid After: 14JUN
19JUN11 Caribbean Air CA 3631		
From: Fort de France, Martinique (FDF)	Departs: 1150A	Business Confirmed
To: Nita City, Nita (Nita City Intern'l)	Arrives: 820P	Fare Basis: TC8BX
		Not Valid Before: 19JUN
		Not Valid After: 19JUN

Form of Payment: Credit Card - Visa - Charged to Jeffrey Potter

Endorsement/Restrictions: Nonref/Change Fee Plus Fare Diff Applies/Valid US Only

Positive Identification Required for Airport Check-In

Carriage and other service provided by the carrier are subject to conditions of carriage, which are hereby incorporated by reference. These conditions may be obtained from the issuing carrier.

Nita Travel Company . . . Your Gateway to Fun in the Sun!

Exhibit 30

NITA TRAVEL COMPANY   eTICKET RECEIPT

Reservation Code:	WQMFKA	Issuing Agent:	Nita City, Nita
Ticket Number:	5996739313271	Issuing Agent:	3BA78/4076
Issuing Airline:	CARIBBEAN AIRLINES	IATA number:	66397478
Date Issued:	30May11	Invoice number:	483228
Customer Number:	2896768575		
Passenger:	Cheryl Tobias		

14JUN11   Caribbean Air CA 1066   Seat 15A

From: Nita City, Nita (Nita City Intern'l)   Departs: 730A   Business Confirmed

To: Fort de France, Martinique (FDF)   Arrives: 355P   Fare Basis: TC8BX

Not Valid Before: 14JUN

Not Valid After: 14JUN

19JUN11   Caribbean Air CA 3631

From: Fort de France, Martinique (FDF)   Departs: 1150A   Business Confirmed

To: Nita City, Nita (Nita City Intern'l)   Arrives: 820P   Fare Basis: TC8BX

Not Valid Before: 19JUN

Not Valid After: 19JUN

Form of Payment: Credit Card - Visa - Charged to Jeffrey Potter

Endorsement/Restrictions: Nonref/Change Fee Plus Fare Diff Applies/Valid US Only

Positive Identification Required for Airport Check-In

Carriage and other service provided by the carrier are subject to conditions of carriage, which are hereby incorporated by reference. These conditions may be obtained from the issuing carrier.

Nita Travel Company . . . Your Gateway to Fun in the Sun!

Martinique Princess Hotel
76 Rue de la Plage
Forte de France, Martinique

Name:	Mr. & Mrs. Jeffrey Potter	Guests: 2
Address:	4920 Thorndale Avenue	Room: 1370
	Nita City, Nita	

Arrival: 6/14/11   Departure: 6/19/11

Date	Description	ID	Ref. No.	Charges	Credits	Balance
6/14/11	Room/Deluxe Suite	MRC	1370	325.00		
6/14/11	I. Room Tax	MIT	1370	29.65		
6/14/11	City Occup. Tax	MOE	1370	10.98		
6/14/11	Room Service	MCH	1370	48.19		
6/15/11	Room/Deluxe Suite	MRC	1370	325.00		
6/15/11	I. Room Tax	MIT	1370	29.65		
6/15/11	City Occup. Tax	MOE	1370	10.98		
6/15/11	Masseuse	MAS	1370	80.50		
6/15/11	Masseuse	MAS	1370	80.50		
6/15/11	Room Service	MCH	1370	28.99		
6/15/11	Room Service	MCH	1370	158.90		
6/16/11	Room/Deluxe Suite	MRC	1370	325.00		
6/16/11	I. Room Tax	MIT	1370	29.65		
6/16/11	City Occup. Tax	MOE	1370	10.98		
6/16/11	Day Spa	MSG	1370	125.29		
6/16/11	Day Spa	MSG	1370	60.13		
6/16/11	Room Service	MCH	1370	33.48		
6/16/11	Laundry Services	MLS	1370	71.17		
6/16/11	Boutique	MBB	1370	148.75		
6/16/11	Room Service	MCH	1370	48.30		
6/16/11	Champagne Cruise	MCC	1370	198.45		
6/16/11	Champagne Cruise	MCC	1370	198.45		
Date	Description	ID	Ref. No.	Charges	Credits	Balance

6/17/11	Room/Deluxe Suite	MRC	1370	325.00
6/17/11	I. Room Tax	MIT	1370	29.65
6/17/11	City Occup. Tax	MOE	1370	10.98
6/17/11	Room Service	MCH	1370	68.90
6/17/11	Tarot Card Reader	MTR	1370	51.50
6/17/11	Masseuse	MAS	1370	80.50
6/17/11	Room Service	MCH	1370	62.99
6/17/11	Day Spa	MSG	1370	75.22
6/17/11	Flower Show	MFB	1370	31.00
6/17/11	Room Service	MCH	1370	79.42
6/17/11	Room Service	MCH	1370	108.14
6/17/11	Movies	MOV	1370	15.00
6/18/11	Room/Deluxe Suite	MRC	1370	325.00
6/18/11	I. Room Tax	MIT	1370	29.65
6/18/11	City Occup. Tax	MOE	1370	10.98
6/18/11	Day Spa	MSG	1370	28.68
6/18/11	Room Service	MCH	1370	43.10
6/18/11	Island Tour	MCL	1370	58.33
6/18/11	Island Tour	MCL	1370	58.33
6/18/11	Room Service	MCH	1370	61.30
6/18/11	Champagne Cruise	MCC	1370	198.45
6/18/11	Champagne Cruise	MCC	1370	198.45
6/19/11	Room Service	MCH	1370	38.95

$4,304.52

I agree that my liability for this bill is not waived and agree to be held personally liable in the event that the indicated person, company, or association fails to pay for any part or the full amount of these charges.

Thank you for being our guest at the Martinique Princess Hotel

Exhibit 33

Madden & James

Suite 720 • Nita Bank Building • Nita City, Nita 99994 • (555) 555-0003

James Barber
Pierce, Johnson & Clark
Nita National Bank Plaza, Nita City, Nita 99994

March 15, 2012

Re: *Potter v. Shrackle and Shrackle Construction Co.*

Jim:

Although I think there is no obligation to do this under the Rules, I thought I would update Jeffrey Potter's answers at his deposition with regard to his relationship with Cheryl Tobias. If asked about that relationship at this point, Mr. Potter would state:

I began a relationship with Cheryl Tobias in the late spring of 2011. That relationship ended in January 2012. The basis for ending the relationship was that I was unable to move on to another long-term relationship after the death of my wife. Cheryl and I agreed it would be better to break off the relationship at that point.

I would be happy to sign a request to admit to this effect.

Sincerely,

William James

SPECIAL IMPEACHMENT PROBLEMS

Problems 1, 2, and 3 are designed to be used in conjunction with the special impeachment slides that come with the PowerPoint slide show in order to learn how to integrate technology into the impeachment process. There are several options for display that accompany the transcript segment for each witness: (1) the written Q and A only; (2) the video only; (3) the video with transcript; (4) a photo taken of the deponent with transcript; and (5) the Q and A revealing one at a time. For Problem 1 the slides are numbers 146–150; Problem 2, 151–155; Problem 3, 156–160.

PROBLEM 1 – JEFFREY POTTER

Assume that Jeffrey Potter is called as a witness for plaintiff and testifies at trial as follows: "She would hear nothing about retiring. She had no interest in it at all."

(a)   For the defendant, cross-examine Potter based upon his deposition.

(b)   For the plaintiff, conduct any necessary redirect examination.

PROBLEM 2 – CHARLES SHRACKLE

Assume that Charles Shrackle is called as a witness for defendant and testifies at trial as follows:

> Q.   What happened after you left Builders Supply?
>
> A.   I called Poe just as I was pulling out of Builders Supply. It must have been about ten after three.
>
> Q.   Did you use your cell phone at any other time before the accident?
>
> A.   No.

(a)   For the plaintiff, cross-examine Shrackle based upon his deposition.

(b)   For the defendant, conduct any necessary redirect examination.

PROBLEM 3 – JAMES MARSHALL

Assume that James Marshall is called as a witness for the plaintiff and testifies as follows:

> Q.   How long was it from the time you first saw the woman walking towards the crosswalk until you heard the thud?
>
> A.   No more than a couple of seconds, maybe five seconds, certainly no more than ten.

(a)   For the defendant, cross-examine Marshall based upon his deposition.

(b)   For the defendant, cross-examine Marshall based upon his handwritten statement.

(c)   For the plaintiff, conduct any necessary redirect examination.

Problem 4 – Marilyn Kelly

Assume that Marilyn Kelly is called as a witness for the plaintiff and testifies at trial as follows:

"At the time of the thud the front of the truck was about halfway through the crosswalk. It was not completely straightened out from making the left turn."

(a)   For the defendant, cross-examine Kelly based upon her deposition.

(b)   For the plaintiff, conduct any necessary redirect examination.

Problem 5 – Alice Mallory

Assume that Alice Mallory is called as a witness for the defendant and testifies at trial as follows:

"When the woman reached the median, she suddenly turned south and began to walk south on the median strip. She had walked at least fifteen or twenty feet south of the crosswalk when I looked down to continue talking to the boy."

(a)   For the plaintiff, cross-examine Mallory based upon her deposition.

(b)   For the defendant, conduct any necessary redirect examination.

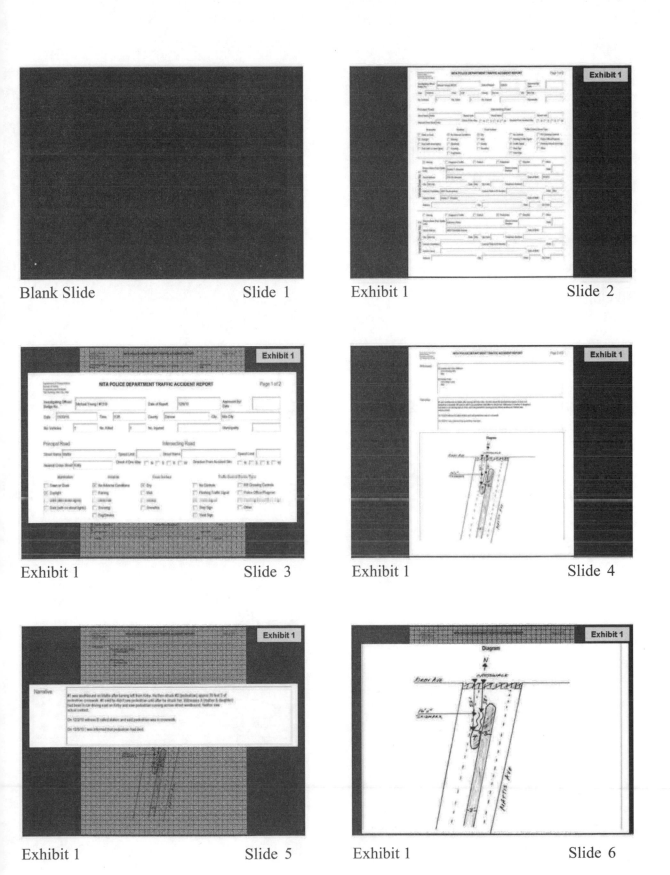

Blank Slide   Slide 1

Exhibit 1   Slide 2

Exhibit 1   Slide 3

Exhibit 1   Slide 4

Exhibit 1   Slide 5

Exhibit 1   Slide 6

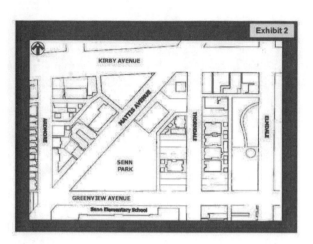

Exhibit 2   Slide 7

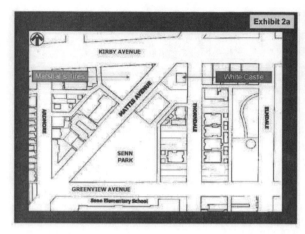

Exhibit 2a   Slide 8

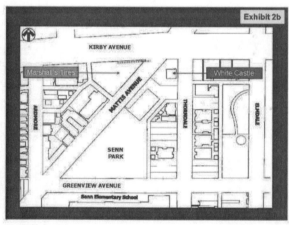

Exhibit 2b   Slide 9

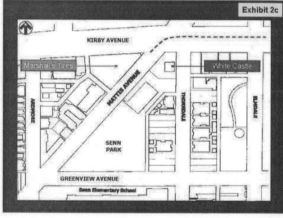

Exhibit 2c   Slide 10

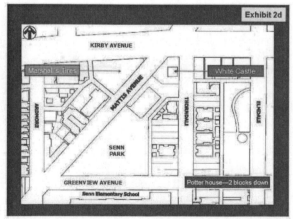

Exhibit 2d   Slide 11

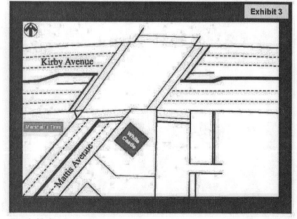

Exhibit 3   Slide 12

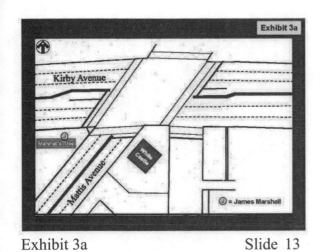

Exhibit 3a   Slide 13

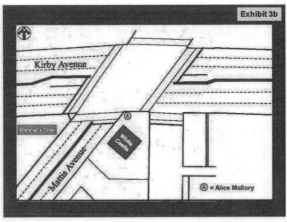

Exhibit 3b   Slide 14

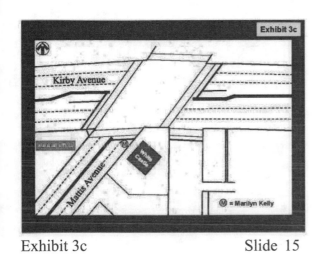

Exhibit 3c   Slide 15

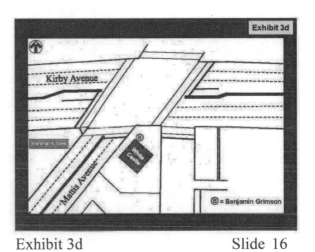

Exhibit 3d   Slide 16

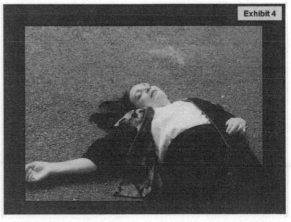

Exhibit 3e   Slide 17

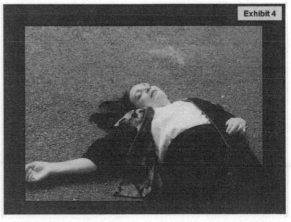

Exhibit 4   Slide 18

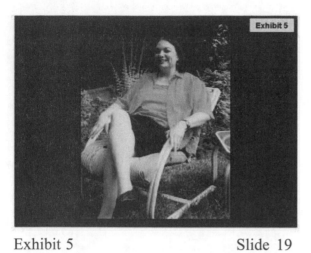

Exhibit 5   Slide 19

Exhibit 6   Slide 20

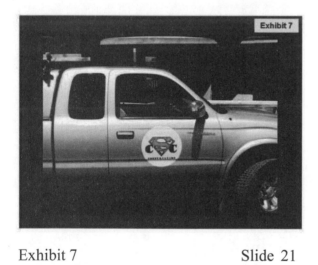

Exhibit 7   Slide 21

Exhibit 7a   Slide 22

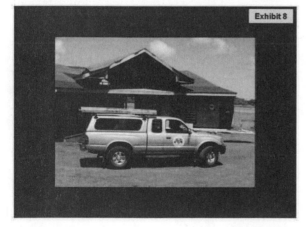

Exhibit 8   Slide 23

Exhibit 9   Slide 24

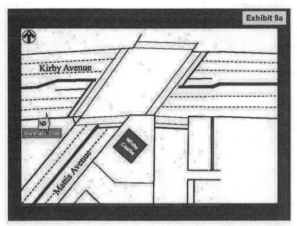

Exhibit 9a   Slide 25

Exhibit 10   Slide 26

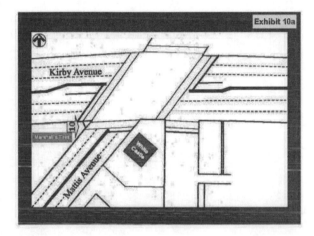

Exhibit 10a   Slide 27

Exhibit 11   Slide 28

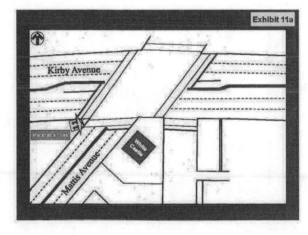

Exhibit 11a   Slide 29

Exhibit 12   Slide 30

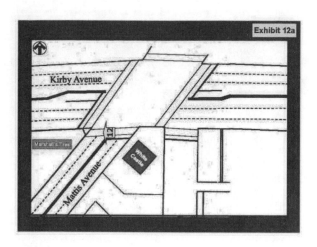

Exhibit 12a   Slide 31

Exhibit 13   Slide 32

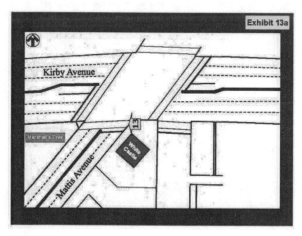

Exhibit 13a   Slide 33

Exhibit 14   Slide 34

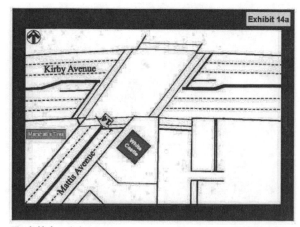

Exhibit 14a   Slide 35

Exhibit 15   Slide 36

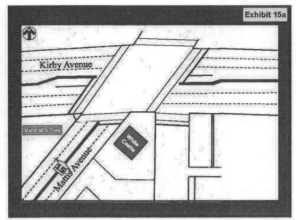

Exhibit 15a   Slide 37

Exhibit 16   Slide 38

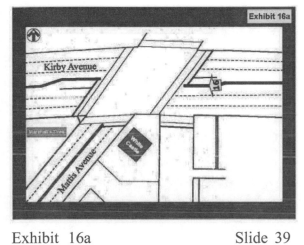

Exhibit 16a   Slide 39

Exhibit 17   Slide 40

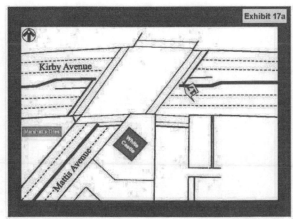

Exhibit 17a   Slide 41

Exhibit 18   Slide 42

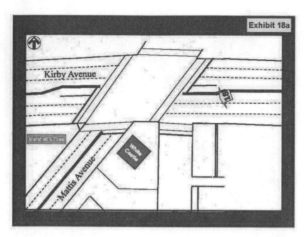

Exhibit 18a   Slide 43

Exhibit 19   Slide 44

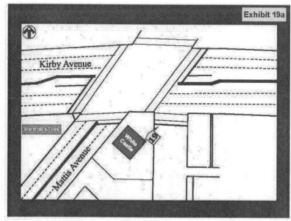

Exhibit 19a   Slide 45

Exhibit 20   Slide 46

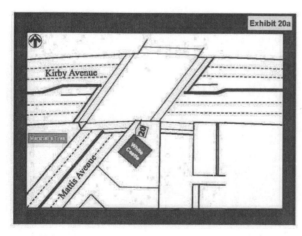

Exhibit 20a   Slide 47

Exhibit 21   Slide 48

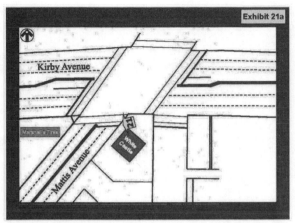

Exhibit 21a   Slide 49

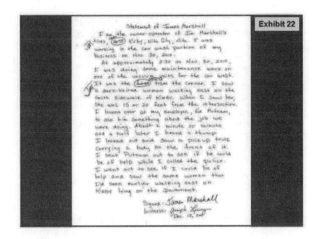

Exhibit 22   Slide 50

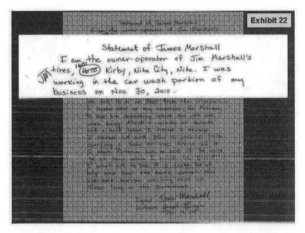

Exhibit 22   Slide 51

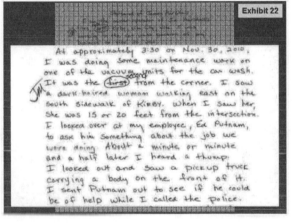

Exhibit 22   Slide 52

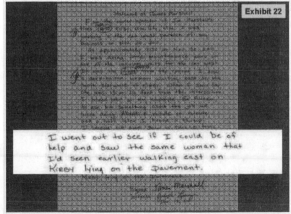

Exhibit 22   Slide 53

Exhibit 23   Slide 54

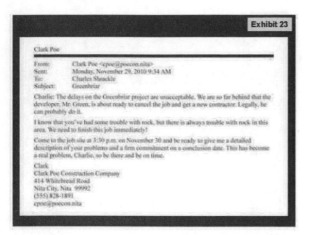

Exhibit 23   Slide 55

Exhibit 23   Slide 56

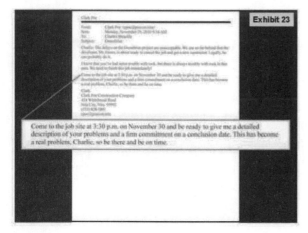

Exhibit 23   Slide 57

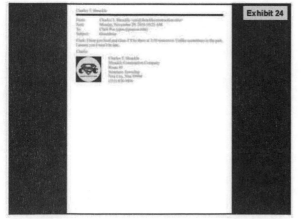

Exhibit 23   Slide 58

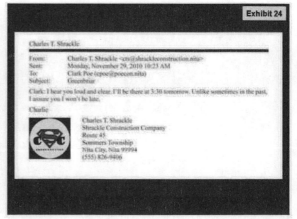

Exhibit 24   Slide 59

Exhibit 24   Slide 60

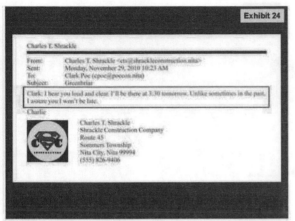

Exhibit 24   Slide 61

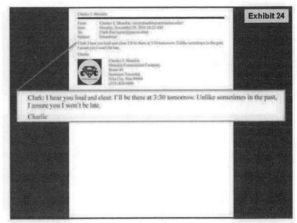

Exhibit 24   Slide 62

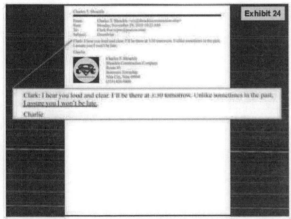

Exhibit 24   Slide 63

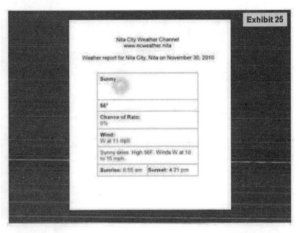

Exhibit 25   Slide 64

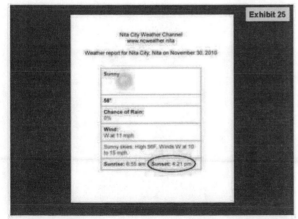

Exhibit 25   Slide 65

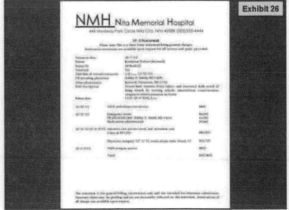

Exhibit 26   Slide 66

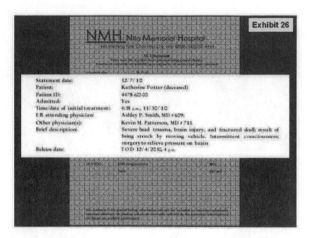

Exhibit 26   Slide 67

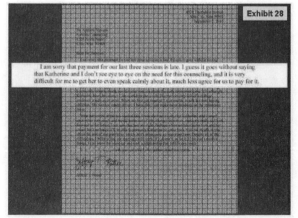

Exhibit 26   Slide 68

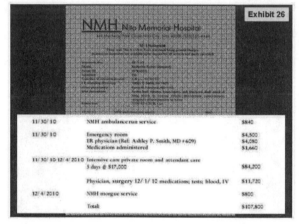

Exhibit 26   Slide 69

Exhibit 27   Slide 70

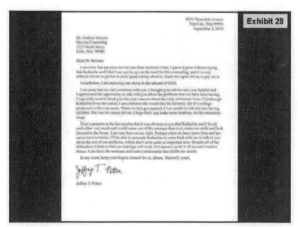

Exhibit 28   Slide 71

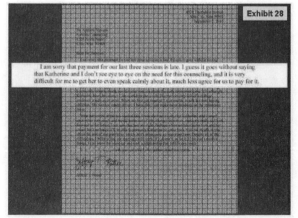

Exhibit 28   Slide 72

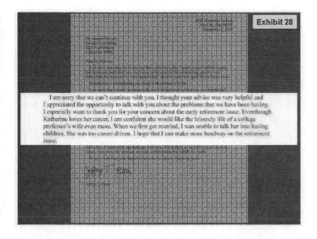

Exhibit 28

I am sorry that we can't continue with you. I thought your advice was very helpful and I appreciated the opportunity to talk with you about the problems that we have been having. I especially want to thank you for your concern about the early retirement issue. Eventhough Katherine loves her career, I am confident she would like the leisurely life of a college professor's wife even more. When we first get married, I was unable to talk her into having children. She was too career-driven. I hope that I can make more headway on the retirement issue.

Exhibit 28 — Slide 73

Exhibit 28

Your comments at the last session that it was obvious to you that Katherine and I loved each other very much and would come out of this stronger than ever, make me smile and look forward to the future. I am sure that you are right. Perhaps when we have more time and her career isn't so hectic, I'll be able to persuade Katherine to come back with me to talk to you about the rest of our problems, which don't seem quite so important now. Despite all of the difficulties, I believe that our marriage will work. If it doesn't, so be it. If we can't resolve things, I can leave the marriage and seek a relationship that fulfils my needs.

Exhibit 28 — Slide 74

Exhibit 29

NITA TRAVEL COMPANY — eTICKET RECEIPT

Exhibit 29 — Slide 75

Exhibit 30

NITA TRAVEL COMPANY — eTICKET RECEIPT

Exhibit 30 — Slide 76

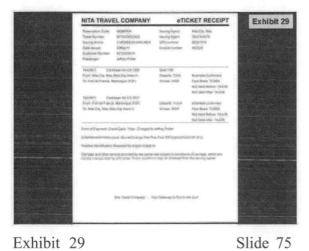

Exhibit 31

Martinique Princess Hotel

Exhibit 31 — Slide 77

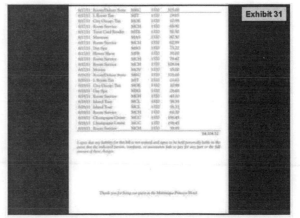

Exhibit 31

Exhibit 31 — Slide 78

Exhibit 32   Slide 79

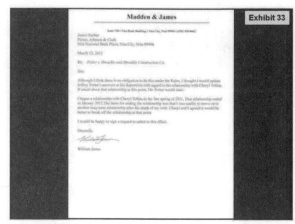

Exhibit 33   Slide 80

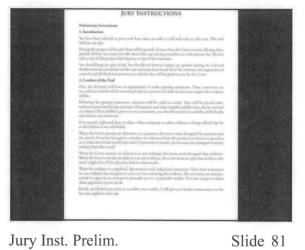

Jury Inst. Prelim.   Slide 81

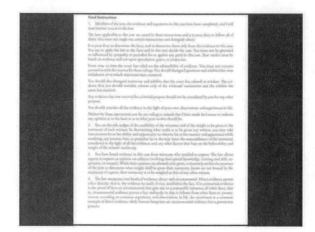

Jury Inst. p. 2   Slide 82

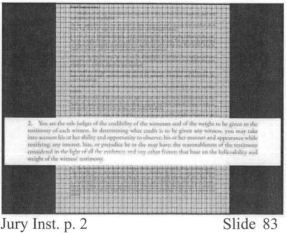

Jury Inst. p. 2   Slide 83

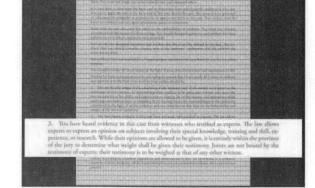

Jury Inst. p. 2   Slide 84

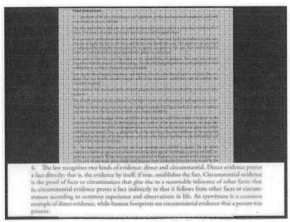

Jury Inst. p. 2   Slide 85

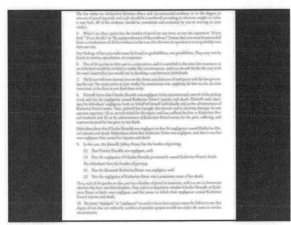

Jury Inst. p. 3   Slide 86

Jury Inst. p. 3   Slide 87

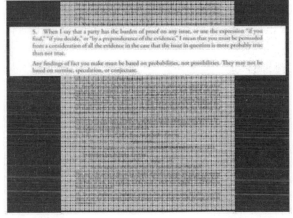

Jury Inst. p. 3   Slide 88

Jury Inst. p. 3   Slide 89

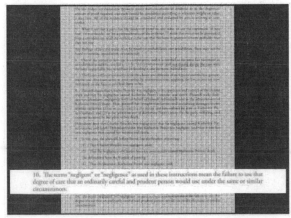

Jury Inst. p. 3   Slide 90

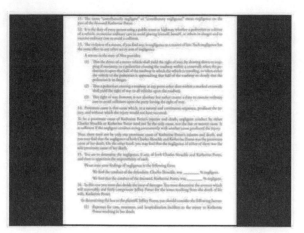

Jury Inst. p. 4 — Slide 91

Jury Inst. p. 4 — Slide 92

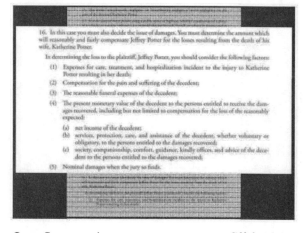

Jury Inst. p. 4 — Slide 93

Jury Inst. p. 4 — Slide 94

Jury Inst. p. 5 — Slide 95

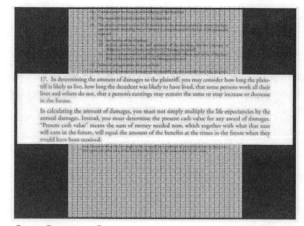

Jury Inst. p. 5 — Slide 96

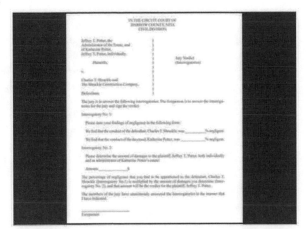

Verdict Form   Slide 97

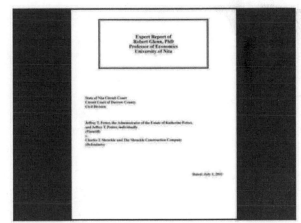

Glenn Report p. 1   Slide 98

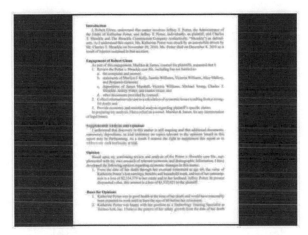

Glenn Report p. 2   Slide 99

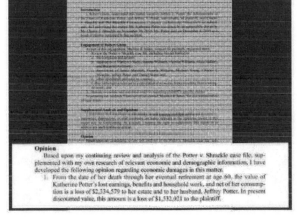

Glenn Report p. 2   Slide 100

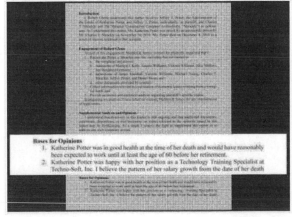

Glenn Report p. 2   Slide 101

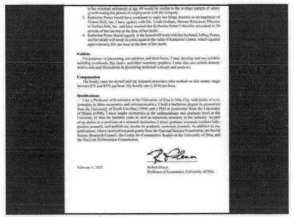

Glenn Report p. 3   Slide 102

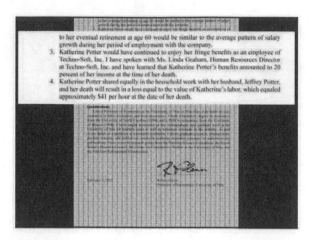

Glenn Report p. 3   Slide 103

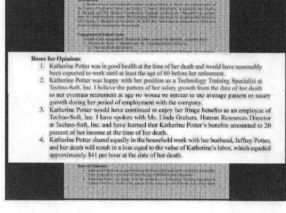

Glenn Report p. 3   Slide 104

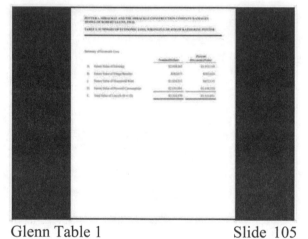

Glenn Table 1   Slide 105

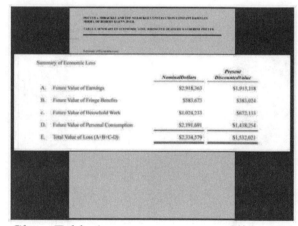

Glenn Table 1   Slide 106

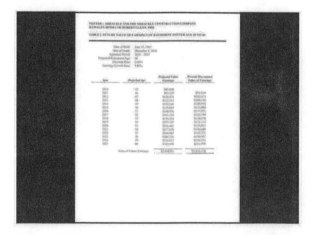

Glenn Table 2   Slide 107

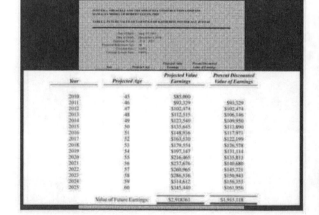

Glenn Table 2   Slide 108

Glenn Table 3 — Slide 109

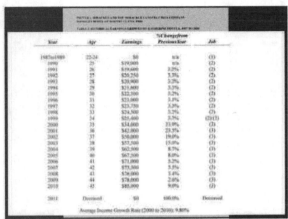

Glenn Table 3 — Slide 110

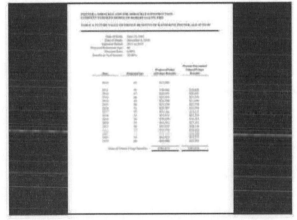

Glenn Table 4 — Slide 111

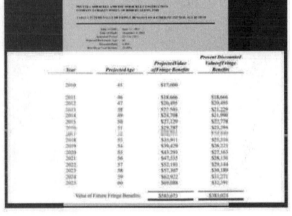

Glenn Table 4 — Slide 112

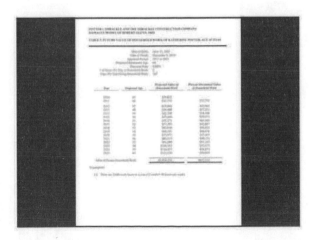

Glenn Table 5 — Slide 113

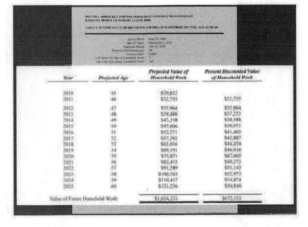

Glenn Table 5 — Slide 114

Glenn Table 6 — Slide 115

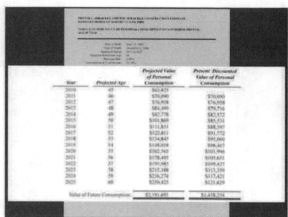

Glenn Table 6 — Slide 116

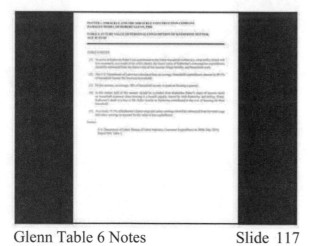

Glenn Table 6 Notes — Slide 117

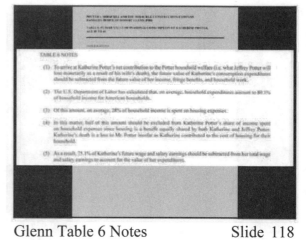

Glenn Table 6 Notes — Slide 118

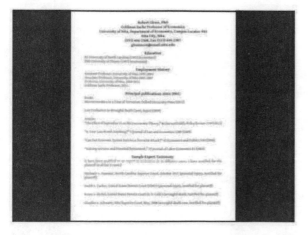

Glenn CV — Slide 119

Buchanan Report — Slide 120

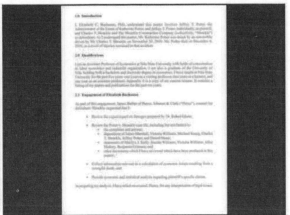

Buchanan Report p. 1 — Slide 121

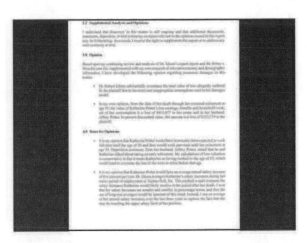

Buchanan Report p. 2 — Slide 122

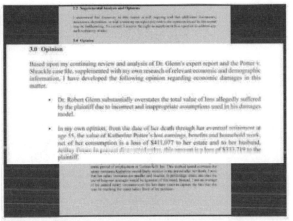

Buchanan Report p. 2 — Slide 123

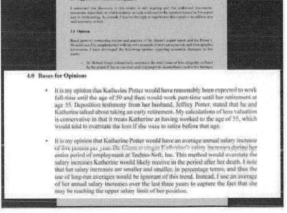

Buchanan Report p. 2 — Slide 124

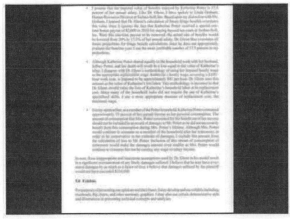

Buchanan Report p. 3 — Slide 125

Buchanan Report p. 3 — Slide 126

Buchanan Report p. 4   Slide 127

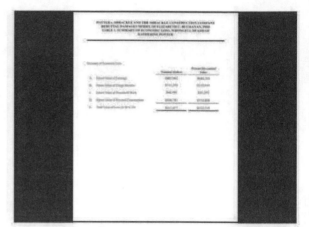

Buchanan Table 1   Slide 128

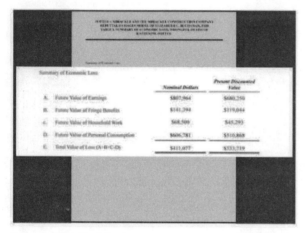

Buchanan Table 1   Slide 129

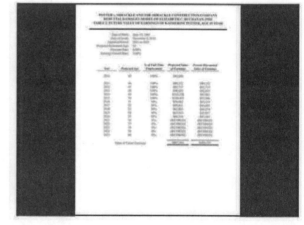

Buchanan Table 2   Slide 130

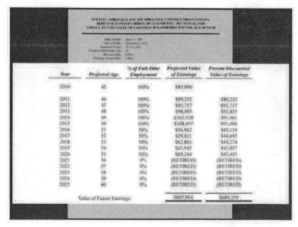

Buchanan Table 2   Slide 131

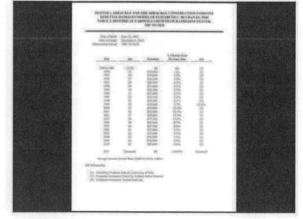

Buchanan Table 3   Slide 132

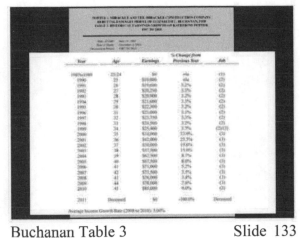

Buchanan Table 3   Slide 133

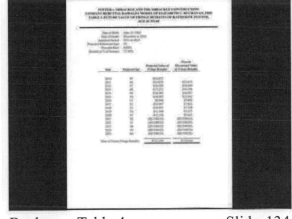

Buchanan Table 4   Slide 134

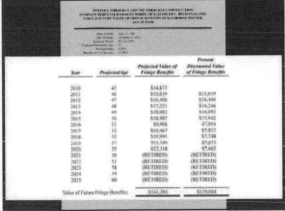

Buchanan Table 4   Slide 135

Buchanan Table 5   Slide 136

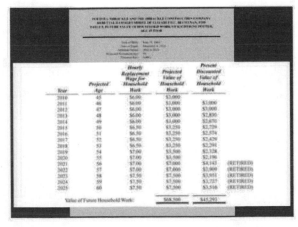

Buchanan Table 5   Slide 137

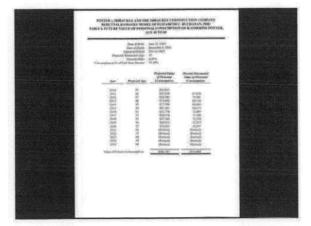

Buchanan Table 6   Slide 138

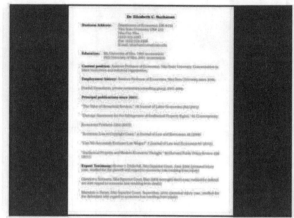

Buchanan Table 6 — Slide 139

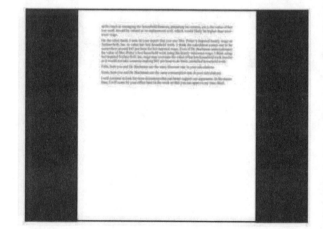

Buchanan CV — Slide 140

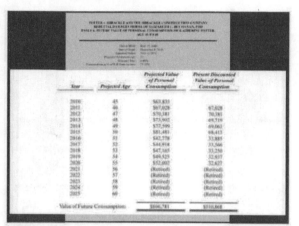

Dyer Memo p. 1 — Slide 141

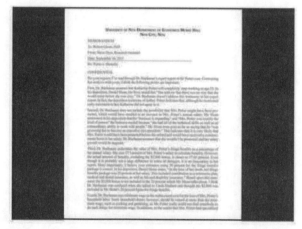

Dyer Memo p. 2 — Slide 142

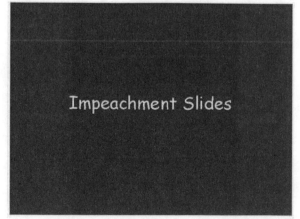

Impeachment Slides — Slide 143

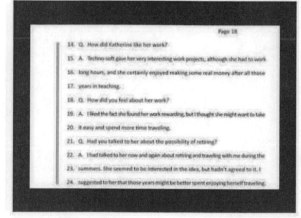

Potter Transcript — Slide 144

Potter Video   Slide 145

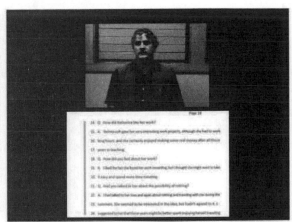

Potter Video   Slide 146
and Transcript

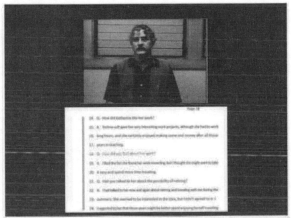

Potter Video   Slide 147
and Transcript

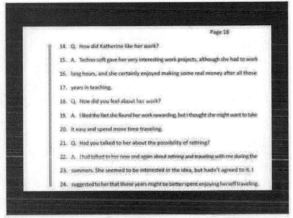

Potter Q & A Reveal   Slide 148

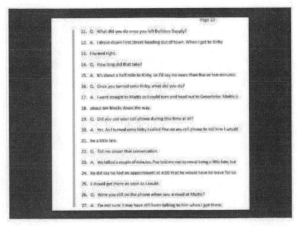

Shrackle Transcript   Slide 149

Shrackle Video   Slide 150

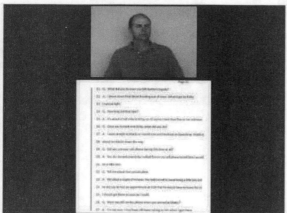

Shrackle Video
and Transcript

Slide 151

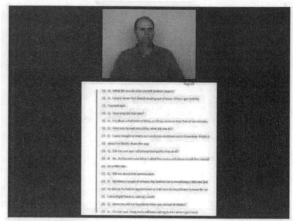

Shrackle Photo
and Transcript

Slide 152

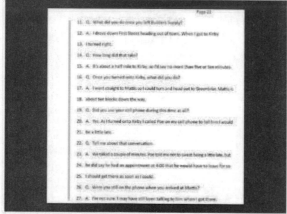
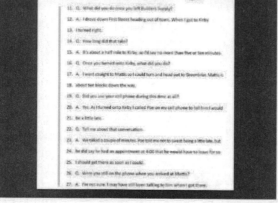

Shrackle Q & A Reveal

Slide 153

Marshall Transcript

Slide 154

Marshall Video

Slide 155

Marshall Video
and Transcript

Slide 156

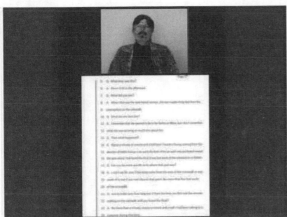

Marshall Photo
and Transcript   Slide 157

Marshall Q & A Reveal   Slide 158

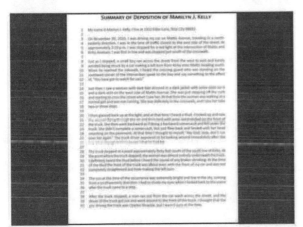

Kelly Depo. p. 1   Slide 159

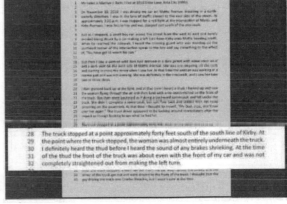

Kelly Depo. p. 1   Slide 160

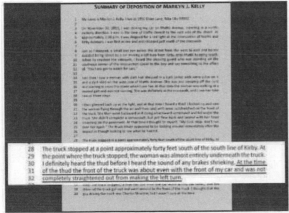

Kelly Depo. p. 1   Slide 161

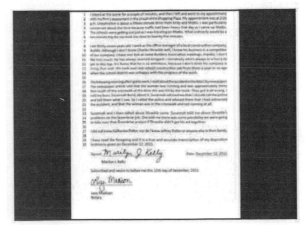

Kelly Depo. p. 2   Slide 162

Mallory Depo. p. 1   Slide 163

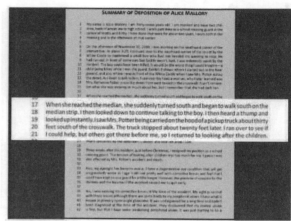

Mallory Depo. p. 1   Slide 164

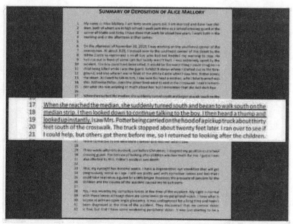

Mallory Depo. p. 1   Slide 165

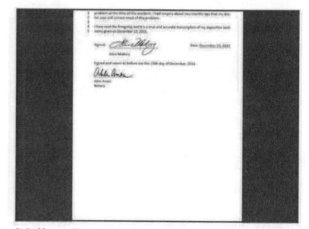

Mallory Depo. p. 2   Slide 166